Step-by-step guide to

Google Sites

By

Barrie "Baz" Roberts

Contents

Introduction **6**

    Restaurant example 6

    Teachers' internal website 7

1 – Setting up a new Google site **8**

2 – Site themes **11**

    Selecting and editing a theme 11

3 – Page headers **15**

    Changing the header type 15

    Changing the header image 17

    Adding an image from your Drive 18

    Changing the page title 20

4 – Inserting text **23**

    Adding text 23

    Changing the text background style 24

    Adding bullet points 26

    Undoing and redoing actions 27

    Previewing your site 28

5 – Adding images **30**

    Changing the section background 34

    Uploading an image 36

6 – Adding new pages **39**

    Adding a new page 39

    Changing the homepage 42

    Duplicating a page 43

    Deleting a page 44

    Adding a subpage 44

    Hiding a page from the navigation 46

    Moving pages within the hierarchy to create or remove subpages 47

    Renaming a page 48

    Filtering the pages in the page menu 49

7 – Adding layouts **50**

    Duplicating pages to use the same layout 56

Adding alt text to make your website more accessible for all 60

Repositioning an image...61

Deleting a layout and adding a new one 65

8 – Adding links to your page **70**

Adding links to other pages to text boxes 70

Linking images and text to other pages 77

Inserting a page divider..82

9 – Adding a Google map...**84**

10 – Adding a calendar and a form **90**

Adding a calendar 90

Adding a reservation form 94

11 – Adding a video **100**

Adding a YouTube video 100

12 – Adding an image carousel **104**

Adding an image carousel..104

Adding alt text to the carousel images. 108

Adding a caption to an image 109

13 – Adding collapsible text **111**

Adding collapsible text..111

14 – Adding a footer **113**

Hiding a footer from a page...114

15 – Publishing your website...**115**

More publishing options 118

Publish settings 118

Sharing published site link 120

16 – Adding a Google Document..**121**

Adding a Google Doc..122

17 – Adding a chart, slides, sheet, and table of contents **124**

Adding a chart from Sheets 124

Adding a Slides presentation 127

Adding a Google Sheet...130

Adding a table of contents...133

18 – Adding a placeholder **135**

19 – Adding buttons..**139**

    Adding buttons 139

    Adding a button to download a PDF of a Google Doc 141

    Duplicating a button 143

    Resizing a button 144

    Changing the colour of the buttons 144

    Linking to an internal webpage 145

20 – Embedding code & games into a page **146**

    Adding a revision game from a website...146

    Adding a game written in Apps Script 151

    Embedding elements as a full page 154

21 – Adding an announcement banner..**157**

22 – Adding links to the menu..**161**

    Adding a new menu section...163

23 – Controlling access to a site **164**

    Giving view rights to a user but not edit rights..166

    More sharing options in Drive 168

    Sharing the draft site with anyone with a link 169

    Sharing with a domain 169

    Reviewing changes to your site before publishing 170

24 – Version history **172**

    Restoring a revision 173

    Naming a revision 173

25 – Duplicating a site **175**

26 – Further settings..**177**

    Navigation bar options..177

    Adding a logo 178

    Adding a favicon 180

    Adding page last updated info 181

    Linking to specific parts of a page 181

    Adding a custom URL..182

    Adding Google Analytics to your site 183

    Adding social media links 183

27 – Using templates **185**

28 – Customise Site Themes **187**

Creating a theme 188

Editing a theme 191

Editing the colours 191

Editing the texts 194

Editing the images 195

Editing the navigation 196

Editing the components 198

Using the styles 199

Duplicating a theme 200

Importing a theme 200

29 – Google Sites help **203**

Final note from the author **204**

Appendix 1 – Setting up a Google account **206**

Introduction

In this book we're going to work through two different real-world projects, where we'll create a website for a bar restaurant and an internal one for a team of teachers.

The beauty of Google Sites is that it's quick and easy to set up a website, it's free, and you can set up both external ones for anyone in the world to view, or restrict it to a specific group of people, useful for internal websites.

As you'll see, it's really easy to create pages and add elements to those pages without any knowledge of coding. It also has the advantage of being connected to Drive and all your files you have on there, which makes sharing those files super easy.

Restaurant example

In this example, we will create a website for a bar restaurant, which will contain the menu, a map of how to find it, a reservation form, a YouTube video of a local event, and a calendar of when those events are.

Teachers' internal website

In this example, we will create a site for a group of teachers, which will give them access to company documents, links to do their attendance on Google Forms via their mobiles, direct access to games, and an easy way to communicate news to them.

You will need a Google account to create a Google site. If you don't already have one, see appendix 1 at the back of the book to see how you create one. It takes two minutes.

Let's get started!

1 – Setting up a new Google site

Setting up a new Google site is really quick and easy and can be done either via Google Drive or a fancy shortcut via Google Chrome. Let's look how to do it from our Google Drive.

First, log in to your Google account and access Drive.

Once in, from your main Drive page, click on the New button.

Then select More and Google Sites.

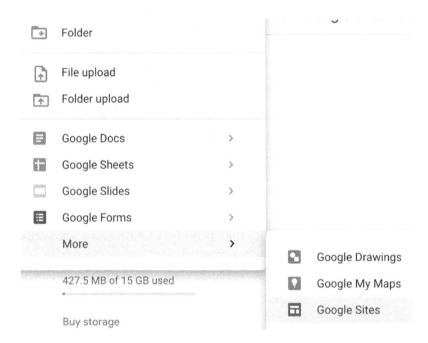

If you've created it in a shared folder, Drive will check if you want to create it in that folder. Just click Create and share, unless you don't want someone to have access to your site.

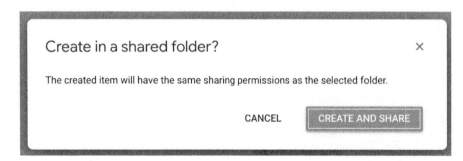

This will open a new window in Chrome (or whatever browser you're using).

And bang! Your blank site is created! How easy was that?!

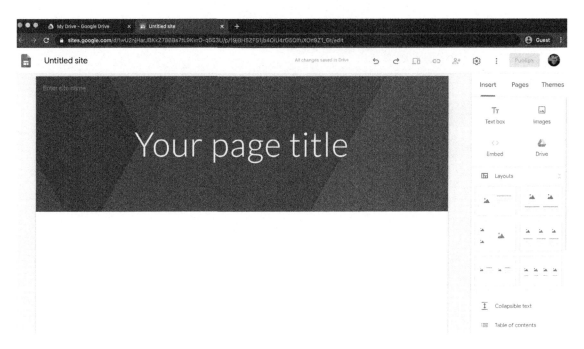

Note, it's still not published yet, but it's ready to the edited.

There is also a shortcut to create a new site. Using Google Chrome, type in the URL: **sites.new** and press enter.

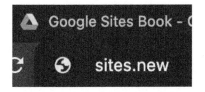

This will create a new site exactly like the one above.

The site won't be saved until you make some changes to the blank.

So, click on the site title at the top of the page, which is currently "Untitled site".

 Untitled site

Then type in the name of your site. Note, this is just the file name, it isn't necessarily the name you'll use once it's published on the internet.

Baz's bar and restaurant

Then press Enter. The site name will also be added to the header.

 Baz's bar and restaurant

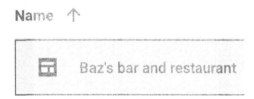

If we go back to Drive we will see that it has added a Sites file.

Name ↑

Baz's bar and restaurant

These can be copied, moved, starred, deleted, just like other Google documents in Drive.

2 – Site themes

In this chapter, we're going to look at changing the whole look of a site by selecting and editing a new theme.

Selecting and editing a theme

Themes change a site's font, colours, and default backgrounds. They affect <u>all</u> the pages of the site, which makes it really quick to change the look of a site, but the downside is that it doesn't allow you to use different fonts on different pages. You can, however, change the backgrounds.

On the right-hand side of the screen, you have most of the editing controls. In the top right-hand corner, you can find the Themes option.

Click on that and you will see a list of the all the themes that are available, with names like Simple, Aristotle, etc.

For each theme, there are 2 options:

1) Change the colours – This affects the background colours of the default headers and some of the features, like underlining and buttons.
2) Font style – There are 3 font options to choose from, and the options will depend on the theme selected.

There are 5 default colours and also a colour picker if you want to select your own colour.

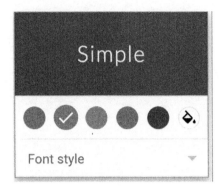

Underneath, you have a drop-down menu to select the font style.

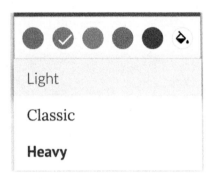

For this theme, we have the choices Light, Classic, and Heavy. The text shows the style they will be.

To select your own colour, click on the colour picker icon on the right-hand side.

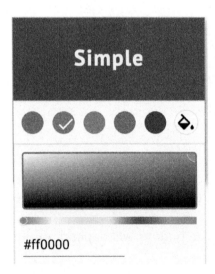

Click on the spectrum of colours to select the hue, i.e. the basic colour. Then click on the shaded rectangle to select how light or dark you want the that colour.

Colours on websites, can also be stated by using a hexadecimal code, e.g. #ff0000. If you know the code you can type it straight into the code box. This can be useful if you have branded colours and need the exact colour.

In the example below I've selected a green colour.

#00ff34

This changes the theme look and also the header you have on that page.

There are a number of themes available which can dramatically change the look of your website.

For my bar restaurant, I'm going to select the Impression theme, select green, and choose the Narrow font style.

3 – Page headers

In this chapter, we're going to look at changing the style of the default header. We'll see how we can add a new background from a list of pre-set images and also how to add our own images from our Drive.

Hover over the header and you will see a menu appear with two options: "Change image" and "Header type".

Changing the header type

First let's look at the options we have with header type. Clicking on Header type, we are presented with 4 options:

Cover, Large banner, Banner (the default), Title only

Clicking on Cover will show a header which will cover the whole page when someone visits our site. They will need to scroll up to see more content.

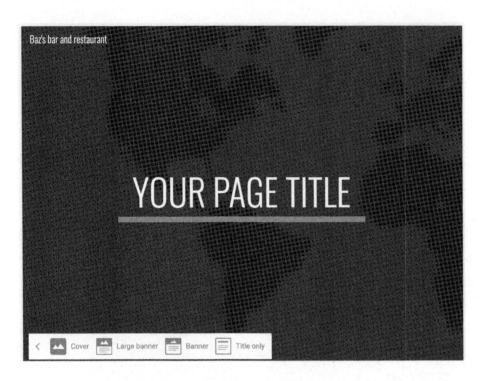

Large banner, is slightly taller than a normal banner.

Banner is the default header type.

And Title only, as the name suggests, just displays the page title without a background image. It takes up the least amount of page height.

Changing the header image

We can also add a different background image to the header. Click on Change image. You have 2 options, one to upload it from your computer, or to select one from different places, like the image gallery, your Drive, etc.

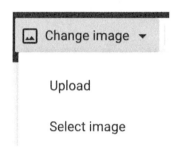

Here, I'm going to select an image from the built-in image gallery. Click Select image. This opens the gallery, then scroll down to the image you want.

Select images

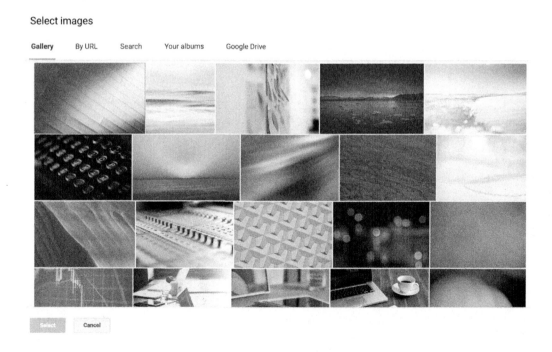

Click on it and then click Select.

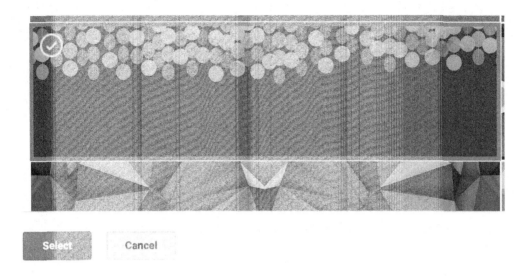

This will replace the default header with this new one.

Automatically, the site will adjust the colours in the image and text so in theory they are more readable. In practice, this doesn't always work. You can turn the readability adjustment on or off, by hovering over the header and in the bottom right-hand corner, clicking on the little stars.

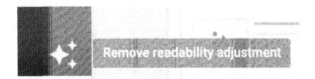

Adding an image from your Drive

This time let's add our own image that's on my Drive. Click on Change image, then click on Google Drive.

Select images

Gallery   By URL   Search   Your albums   Google Drive

Find the image you want, click on it and click Select.

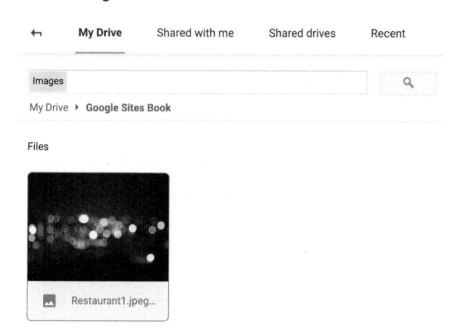

The header is now using the image.

Changing the page title

Now, let's give the page a title. Double-click on the text and type in the name you want.

You also have some basic editing options.

You can select different text styles, add bolding or italics, orientate the text horizontally, add a link, remove any text formatting, or delete it.

The text styles are: normal text, title, heading, sub-heading, and small. As this is a page title, I'm going to leave it on Title.

I also want to centre the text, so choose the centre option.

The text I've written is a bit big for the text box and causes it to go on two lines, which is not what I want. So, I need to make the text box wider.

Just click and drag the blue circle on the left-hand side of the box to the left and for the blue circle on the right-hand side of the box, drag it to the right. In other words, making the box wider.

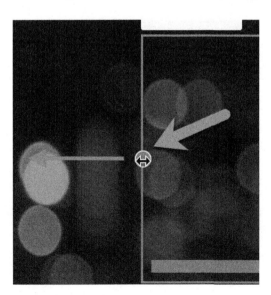

And finally, I'll make the text bold. Note, you choose the font style in the theme but also have some more control over the look by editing the text box.

Now, we have our header for the homepage.

4 – Inserting text

In this chapter, we're going to learn how to:

- add different types of text via text boxes
- change the background style of the text block
- add bullet points
- undo or redo any of our actions.

So far, we've added a header to our homepage. Now, let's add some text welcoming our customers and giving them an overview of the restaurant.

Adding text

There are two ways to add text:

1) Go to the sidebar and click on Insert (if not already selected) and then Text box.

This will add a horizontal block under the header and add a text box within it.

2) The other way is to <u>double click</u> on the page in the blank white space under the header. This will bring up a circle menu where you can then click the TT icon, to open the same text box as above.

Personally, I find the second way the quickest to use, especially when adding lots of different text sections.

In the text box, type the text you want.

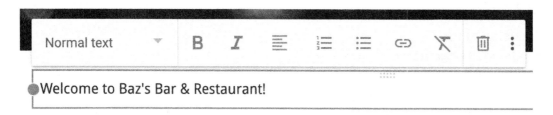

By default the style is "normal text". To change that, click on the drop-down menu, "Normal text". This presents you with different text styles.

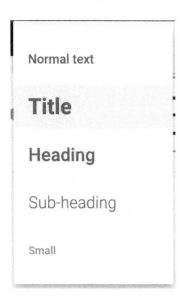

For this page, I'm going to select Header and as you can see it's changed the style of the text to be all in capitals and to be a little bit bigger.

As we saw with the header options, you can also add bolding, italics, change the horizontal orientation, add a link, remove any formatting, or delete the text box.

Changing the text background style

To the left of the block, there are 3 options:

Change background style, duplicate the block, delete the block.

To change the background style, click on the palette icon. This brings up 4 options:

1) Standard style – this is the default normal blank text box with no background
2) Emphasis 1 – This adds a light background to the block
3) Emphasis 2 – This adds a stronger background, usually a colourful one, based on the theme chosen
4) Image – You can upload your own background image

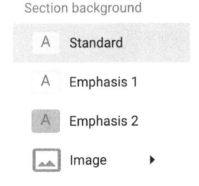

Here's the Emphasis 1 option chosen:

But I think I'm going to go for the strong green Emphasis 2 option as this is the welcome message to my customers.

So, the page now looks like this:

Next, let's add a sub heading and a tagline. Under the text box we just created, in the white space, I double click to open the circle edit menu and select TT (text box). I type in the text and select Sub-heading from the menu. This produces slightly larger type with the theme colour.

Adding bullet points

Next I create another text box underneath and here I want to give some basic information about my restaurant. I type in the text and this time I also want to add some bullet points, so after writing the first line, I click on the bullet point icon from the menu. Note, next to it, it's also possible to add a numbered list.

Baz's Bar & Restaurant offers the best food in Seville.

- A relaxing environment
- 5-star quality fresh food
- The best Cruzcampo beer in town

The page now looks like this:

Baz's bar and restaurant

BAZ'S BAR & RESTAURANT

WELCOME TO BAZ'S BAR & RESTAURANT!

A place to enjoy great food

Baz's Bar & Restaurant offers the best food in Seville.
- A relaxing environment
- 5-star quality fresh food
- The best Cruzcampo beer in town

Undoing and redoing actions

Finally, while you're editing your page, and you do something you didn't want to do, don't worry Sites remembers all the edits and you can easily undo the last one. Just click on the backwards arrow at the top of the page. To redo it, select the forward arrow.

Undo last action

We will see in a future chapter, that it's possible to go back to a certain revision of your page, just like you can in Google Sheets, Docs, etc.

Previewing your site

So far we've seen our site in the edit mode but we can preview what it looks like not only on a computer, but on other devices like a tablet and a mobile. Google Sites is responsive, which means it will automatically adjust the layout and its look depending on what device the viewer is using.

At the top of the screen, click on the Preview icon.

This will bring up the preview of the site. In the screenshot below, it's what it will look like on a computer.

In the bottom corner you have a floating menu with different view options. From left to right, you can preview the site as if it were on a mobile, a tablet, or a computer. Just click on the icon to change the view.

This is the tablet view:

And this is the mobile view:

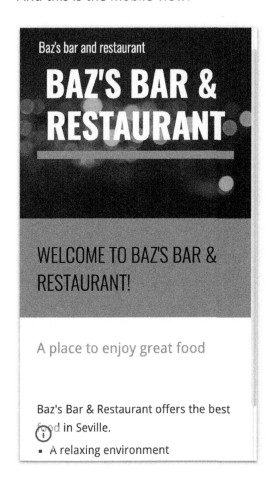

As you can see it looks good in all three.

5 – Adding images

In this chapter, we're going to look at how we add images to our website. In our example site, we're going to add an image just below the welcome message and also an image at the bottom of the page after the text.

We're going to look at inserting them, moving them, and changing the background.

To start, double click on an empty space on the page to bring up the circle menu. Then click the red image icon.

Baz's Bar & Restaurant offers the best food in Seville.

- A relaxing environment

- 5-star quality fresh food

- The best Cruzcampo beer in town

This opens the Select Images dialogue box. By default, it will open our recent photos on our Drive. You can also search for an image via a URL, in Google images or Photos.

To be honest, I generally only use two methods, either I add images stored on my Drive or I upload them directly from my computer. These are the two methods we'll look at in detail in this chapter.

Find the image you want. Note you can use the search box of you know the title of the image, or you can look for it by clicking on My Drive and going to the folder it is in.

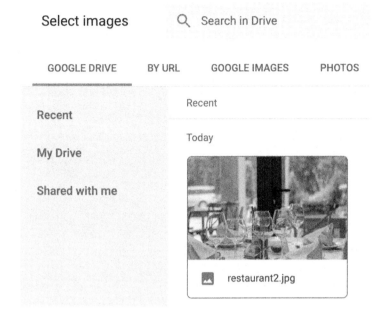

Either just double click on the image to add it, or click on it and then click Insert.

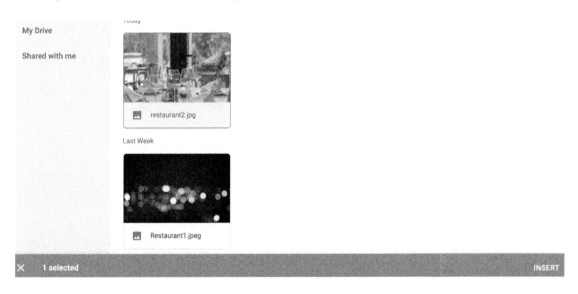

This will add the image on your webpage. At the moment, it is the right size and it's not in the place I want it. Click on the image.

A place to enjoy great food

With the mouse button held down, you can drag it to where you want with the block. You will see guidelines appear to help you position it correctly.

Here I'm going to position it in the middle of the page and as you can see it's further added blue positioning lines to show me that it's in the middle of the page.

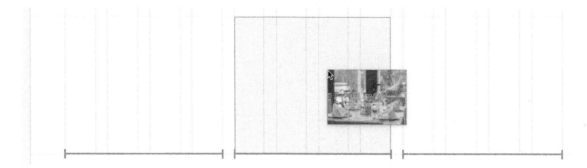

Just let the mouse button go to drop it into place.

The image is a bit small, so I'm going to resize it so it fits the page width. Click on one of the blue dots on the size of the image and drag it sideways so that it fits the width.

The image has now been automatically cropped and it's chopped the top and bottom of my image. That's easily remedied. There is an edit toolbar that appears when you click on the image.

Click on the second icon to uncrop it.

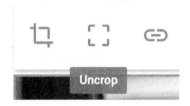

As you can see it's resized the image, whilst still fitting the width.

Changing the section background

I want to add the above image below the welcome text and that text has a green background, which we added earlier by changing the background to Emphasis 2. Well, we can do the same with images.

To the side of the image block, you have the section background palette icon. Click on that.

Now, as we saw with the welcome message, let's select Emphasis 2. Note, we have the same options as a text box background.

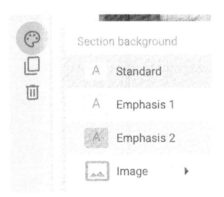

This has now added the green background.

Now we need to move it to below the welcome message. Just to the right of the 3 icons on the left-hand side of the block, you will see some grey dots. Click and hold on these then drag it to move the block upwards or downwards.

As you move the block, you will see a blue line under the block above. This is to show you where the block will be placed when you let the mouse button go. Here I'm going to place it under the welcome message.

As you can see, the image is now under the welcome message and you can see the background appears to be the just one for both blocks, even though in reality it's two separate blocks.

Uploading an image

If we don't have the images already stored on our Drive, we can also upload them straight from our computer.

To do so, double click on a blank part of the page to open the circle insert menu. Then click on the green Upload icon, which is a cloud with an upwards arrow.

This then opens your file manager on your computer. You find the file you want and click Open. Note, you can open multiple files if you want and these will be added in different positions on the page.

As you can see it's added the image, although it's above the text and I want it to be below it.

A place to enjoy great food

Baz's Bar & Restaurant offers the best food in Seville.

- A relaxing environment
- 5-star quality fresh food
- The best Cruzcampo beer in town

We click on the block and drag it until we see the blue line under the text. Then drop it there.

Baz's Bar & Restaurant offers the best food in Seville.

- A rel
- 5-sta
- The

We now have the image at the bottom, and I've resized it so it fits the width of the page.

Baz's Bar & Restaurant offers the best food in Seville.

- A relaxing environment
- 5-star quality fresh food
- The best Cruzcampo beer in town

There are more ways to work with images and we will look at those in future chapters.

6 – Adding new pages

So far we've made one webpage, but of course most websites contain multiple pages. In this chapter, we're going to create a new page which will show our menu, and we will cover the following page options:

- Adding a new page
- Duplicating a page
- Deleting a page
- Hiding a page from the navigation
- Making a page the homepage
- Renaming pages
- Filtering pages

Adding a new page

To add a new page, click on the Pages tab on the sidebar. This will show you that at the moment, we only have a homepage. To add a new page, hover over the plus button at the bottom.

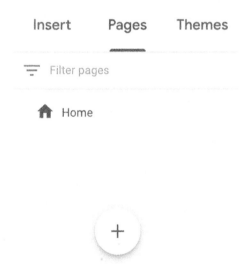

When you do that, it shows four options:

1) To add a new page
2) To add a new link
3) To embed code as a full page
4) To add a new menu section

Click on the New page button.

A little dialogue box will open asking you to name your new page.

New page

Name

_____

Advanced ▾   Done

Type in the name and click Done.

New page

Name

Menu
_____

Advanced ▾   Done

As you can see, it's added the new page. Note, this is on the same level as the homepage. What that means is that it isn't a sub page of the homepage, so is a page separate from it.

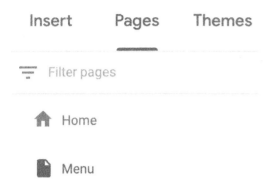

We can see it's created the Menu page and uses the same header and font as the homepage. This we can change if we want.

In the top right-hand corner, we can also see that the navigation bar has appeared and gives us the possibility of navigating to the homepage or the menu page by clicking on their names.

So, it's set up all of this just with a couple of clicks of the mouse!

On the sidebar, we have further page options. Hover over the Menu page and you will see 3 dots appear to the right. This is the options menu for that page.

Click on that and you will be presented with various options.

Set as homepage

Duplicate page

Properties

Add subpage

Hide from navigation

Delete

Changing the homepage

You can change the homepage to the page you've selected. So, for example, you may want people to go straight to the menu page if they enter your general website address, saving them having to navigate to it.

To do so, click on Set as homepage.

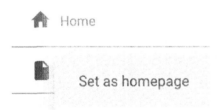

This will add the house icon to the Menu page, meaning that this will be the homepage.

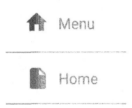

I'm going to press Ctrl+Z to undo that, as I want my customers to go to the homepage with the welcome message first.

Duplicating a page

A quick way to create new pages that are similar is to create one and then duplicate it, then edit whatever is different. This saves you a lot of time in editing and formatting your new page.

Click on the page you want to duplicate and click Duplicate page.

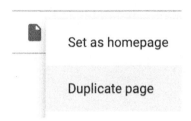

This opens the Duplicate page dialogue box.

Duplicate page

Name

Copy of Menu

Advanced ▼   Done

Like we saw with a new page, just add the name of the page and click Done.

Duplicate page

Name

Menu 2

Advanced ▼   Done

As you can see it's added a new page in the page hierarchy.

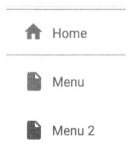

🏠 Home

📄 Menu

📄 Menu 2

Deleting a page

I actually don't want another page yet, so I'm going to delete it. This is easy to do, just click on the page in the menu you want to get rid of and click Delete.

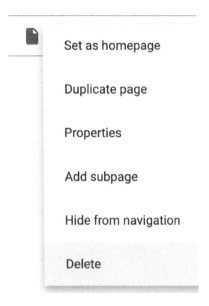

Adding a subpage

Sometimes we want a page to be connected to another page in a hierarchical kind of structure. For example, we may want to have a main menu page but then have the starters, main courses, and desserts as 3 subpages off that main page.

-Menu -Starters
        -Main courses
        -Desserts

This is useful for a couple of reasons. Firstly, if you have a large site it helps you group your pages, making it easier to know what's where. Secondly, it will be easier for the user to find the page, as the pages will be grouped together in the navigation bar.

Click on the page in the menu you want to add a submenu to, then from the 3-dot menu, click on Add subpage.

Set as homepage

Duplicate page

Properties

Add subpage

This will open the new subpage dialogue box. Enter the new of the new subpage and click Done.

New subpage

Name

Starters|

Advanced ▾   Done

As you can see, this has added a subpage called Starters to the Menu page.

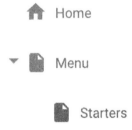

🏠 Home

▾ 📄 Menu

     📄 Starters

In the navigation bar now, we have the Menu page and an arrow, which when we hover over it will show the subpages connected to that page. In this case, the Starters one, which the customer can click on to navigate to that page.

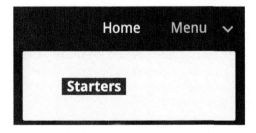

Hiding a page from the navigation

There are times when you don't want to show all the pages to your site users. Either these could be pages which you just don't want them to see, or they could be a work in progress.

Although it could be because you just want to simplify the navigation bar and you will give them other ways to navigate to the pages, for example, by clicking on a button on the page. We'll see in a later chapter.

To hide a page in the navigation, click on the page in the menu you want to hide, click on the 3 dots, and select Hide from navigation.

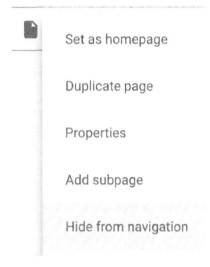

Here I've hidden the Starters menu and as you can see it has a line through it, showing that it's not visible to the site user.

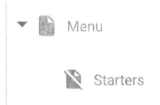

We can see that the page has been removed from the navigation bar too, and we are left with only the homepage and Menu page.

If we also hid the Menu page now, we see that the page is hidden as we saw earlier.

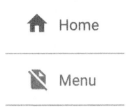

But this time, we also see that it has also removed the navigation bar, as we are now left with only the homepage.

Moving pages within the hierarchy to create or remove subpages

Pages aren't fixed in their position once we make them, we can move them around afterwards. So, we can make a page a subpage and vice-versa, or move a page to a different section of the site.

To move a page, click on the page in the side menu and drag it to its new position. So, here I want to move the Menu page so it's a submenu of the homepage. So, I drag it on top of that page, then release the mouse button.

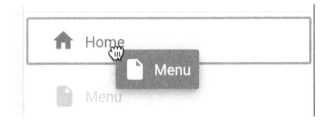

This then changes it to being a submenu of the homepage.

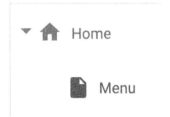

We can see it has also updated the navigation bar accordingly.

To move the Menu page back to being a separate page, I need to drag it to the bottom, where a blue line will appear.

When I release the mouse button there, it will move the page to being on the same level as the homepage, as it was before.

Renaming a page

As well as changing the position of your pages, you can also change the name of your pages. Click on the page in the menu you want to change, and click on the 3-dot menu and then Properties.

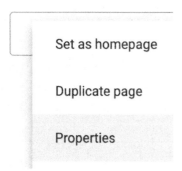

Then delete the current name and add the new one and click Done.

Properties

Name

Starters|
_____

Advanced ▼   Done

Filtering the pages in the page menu

When you have a larger site, you may have lots of lots of pages and it may be more difficult to find the page you want. Fortunately, there's a filter in the Page menu, which will show just the pages that match the letters or words you enter.

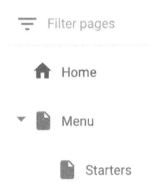

Here I've typed 'st' and it's found the Starters menu. Note, it also shows the page it's connected to, in this case the menu one.

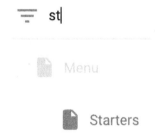

Tip: This can also be useful for editing multiple pages, which have a similar name. For example, you may have a number of pages called menu followed by a number, and you want to edit them one by one but they may be located in different parts of your site. Typing in menu, will show all of those pages, so you can quickly edit them.

7 – Adding layouts

In this chapter, we're going to learn how to use layouts and how they make it much quicker to add images and text in a structured way.

I'm going to add 3 pages which will be my menu, one page for each course: starters, main meals, and desserts.

Let's start on the Starters page. Click on Insert on the sidebar and go to the Layouts section. Here you have various pre-set layouts which add the relevant blocks you need to edit on the page.

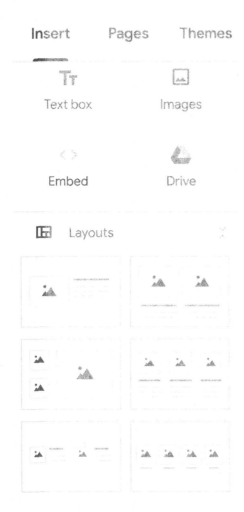

I'm going to choose the 3 images and pieces of texts, as I have 3 starters to add. Click on the layout.

This adds it to the page, ready to be edited. The pluses are where images can be added (and some other content types). Below are headings to describe the images, and below those some additional text.

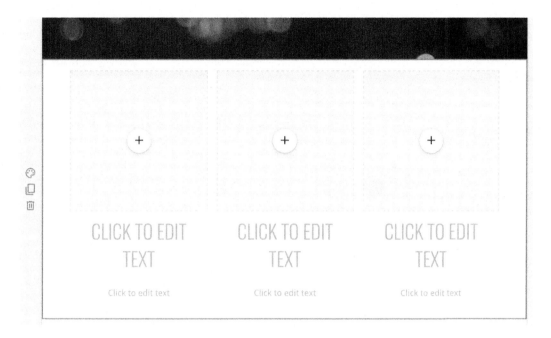

Let's start by editing the first heading. Click on where it says "Click to edit text" on the left.

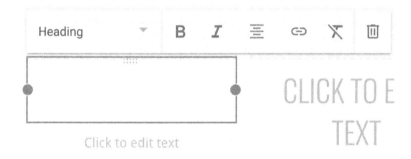

Add the text you want. Note, this by default is a heading, but you could change the text type.

Next let's add the price underneath. This is a normal text box, but again you could change the text type here too.

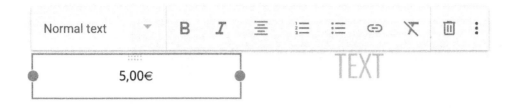

Here's what the text looks like.

MIXED SALAD

5,00€

I do the same for all three starters, which leave it like this:

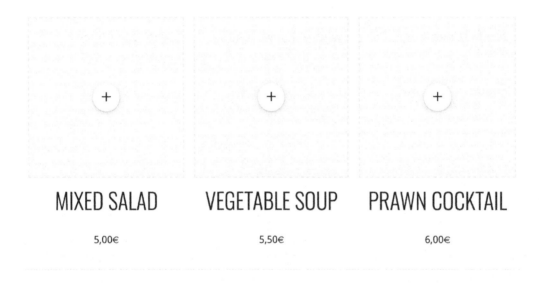

MIXED SALAD	VEGETABLE SOUP	PRAWN COCKTAIL
5,00€	5,50€	6,00€

OK, now I need to add the images of the dishes. Click on the first plus button, here it's for the mixed salad.

This gives you various options:

You can upload an image from your computer, select one from your Drive and the internet, add a file from your Drive, add a YouTube video, a Google calendar, or a Google map.

Most of these we will see in later chapters, but for now, I'm going to add an image from my Drive, so I click Select image.

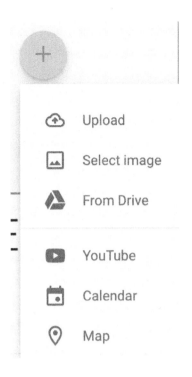

This opens the Select image dialogue we saw earlier. As I've recently uploaded the images I want to use, and can find them in Google Drive > Recent.

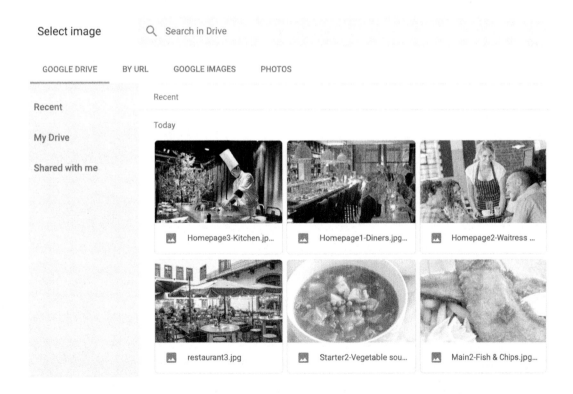

Double-click on the image you want to add it, or click on it and click Insert.

This has added the image of the mixed salad and by default it fills the square placeholder.

I want all my images to be the same size, so I'm going to keep the square template, but if you want to use the original format of the image, click the uncrop icon (the second on the toolbar) and this will return it back to its original size.

With the text it looks like this:

MIXED SALAD

5,00€

I do the same for the other dishes and the page looks like this:

It's starting to look like a proper website now!

Duplicating pages to use the same layout

I now want to have a page for the main courses and as there will be 3 main courses, I will use the same layout as the Starters page. So, rather than creating a page from scratch, I just need to duplicate the Starters page and edit it.

From the Pages menu, click on the page and the 3-dot menu.

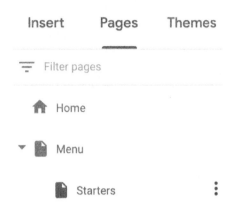

Then click Duplicate page.

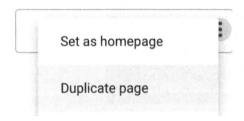

Type in the name of the new page and click Done.

Duplicate page

Name

Main courses

Advanced ▾   Done

As you can see it's added the new page as a subpage of the Menu page.

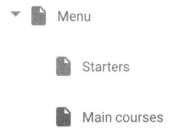

Menu

Starters

Main courses

First, click on the page header and change it to what you want.

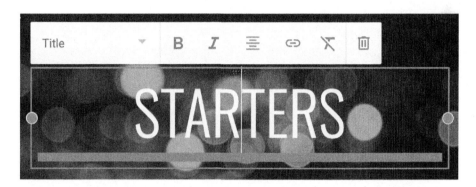

Next edit the images and texts.

MIXED SALAD

5,00€

Just double click on the texts to edit them.

CHICKEN TIKKA MASALA

To replace the current image, click on it and click on the 3 dots in the toolbar.

You have the choice of uploading an image from your computer or select an image from your Drive, as we saw before. As all my images are on my Drive, I click Replace image and Select image.

I find my image and double-click on it to add it.

So, now I have my first main course ready.

CHICKEN TIKKA MASALA

10,00€

Adding alt text to make your website more accessible for all

We should always make our websites accessible for all and Sites has the option, for those who have trouble reading and use screen readers, to add text which describes the image, as they may not be able to see the image.

To add it, click on the image, click on the 3-dot menu and click Add alt text.

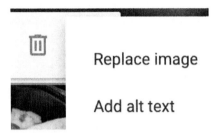

Replace image

Add alt text

A dialogue box will prompt you for the text.

Alt text

Alt text is accessed by screen readers for people who might have trouble seeing your content

┌─ Description ─────────────────────────────┐
│ | │
│   │
└──┘

☐ This is a decorative image

CANCEL   APPLY

Add a description that accurately describes the image, then click Apply.

If it's just a decorative image and serves no specific purpose like choosing what to eat, then click the "This is a decorative image" box.

Alt text

Alt text is accessed by screen readers for people who might have trouble seeing your content

┌─ Description ────────────────────────┐
│   │
│ Chicken Tikka Masala curry│   │
│   │
└──────────────────────────────────────┘

☐ This is a decorative image

                    CANCEL   APPLY

Repositioning an image

Here I've added an image of one of the dishes but as the original photo wasn't in square format, it hasn't cropped it the way I would like. Fortunately, we can move the image around to centre it on the part we want.

Click on the image and then on the crop icon (the first one on the toolbar).

We have two ways we can edit the image:

1) Zoom in and out of the image
2) Move the image around

First, I'm going to zoom in a little. I move the little circle in the bar above the image to the right towards the tick.

The circle changes to blue to show that the zoom has changed.

Next, I click and drag the image to centre it the way I want.

Once I'm happy with the new position, I click the Tick.

So, now we have the main courses set up. The only problem is that the text for the first dish is long and goes onto two lines, which then means it doesn't line up well with the other dishes.

CHICKEN TIKKA
MASALA

FISH N CHIPS

ROAST LAMB

11,50€

12,00€

10,00€

There are different solutions for this. We could use a smaller text type, like a sub heading, or we could use a shorter phrase for the first dish.

Another way is to edit the other two so they line up with the first one. Click on the text of the second dish.

11,50€

Press Enter to add a new line. You will see that this new line is Normal text, and therefore, isn't very tall, so the prices don't line up.

CHICKEN TIKKA
MASALA

10,00€

11,50€

So, change that line to a sub-heading to make it taller. Now you can see it lines up better.

CHICKEN TIKKA
MASALA

FISH N CHIPS

10,00€   11,50€

We do the same for the third dish and now the three line pretty well, whilst keeping the original style.

CHICKEN TIKKA
MASALA

FISH N CHIPS

ROAST LAMB

10,00€   11,50€   12,00€

Deleting a layout and adding a new one

On the third menu page, we're going to add 2 desserts, which means I will have to change the layout to one with just 2 images and texts.

We'll start by duplicating the previous page and then edit it. So, click on the Main courses page and then the 3-dot menu.

Then click Duplicate page.

Set as homepage

Duplicate page

Give it a new name and click Done.

Duplicate page

Name

Desserts

Advanced ▾   Done

Now we have our third menu page.

▼ 📄 Menu

    📄 Starters

    📄 Main courses

    📄 Desserts

Edit the page title.

Next, I want to delete the previous layout. Hover over the layout block and you'll see the trash can on the left-hand side. Click on that to delete it.

Delete the section

CHIC|

Incidentally, if I wanted to duplicate the layout to say show 6 dishes, I would just need to click the duplicate icon (in the middle) and edit the new row.

So, that's now deleted the layout.

Go to the Insert menu and click on the 2-image layout.

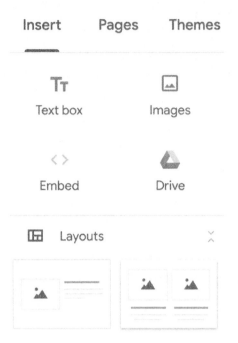

As you can see the layout is similar to the 3 image one.

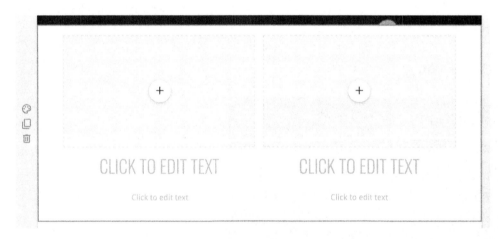

I've added the images and text as before and the page looks like this:

CHEESECAKE

6,00€

APPLE PIE

5,50€

Plus we can see in the navigation bar it's added the 3 subpages to the menu page.

8 – Adding links to your page

One of the key parts of a website is the navigation to different pages. As we've seen in the early chapters, when we add new pages, it updates the navigation menu automatically. We can also add links directly on our pages to pages within our website or to external sites.

In this chapter, we're going to add links on the Menu page to the Starts, Main courses, and Desserts pages.

First, we're going to add links to text boxes, and then we're going to improve this by adding links to images as well, which will have a more professional feel.

Adding links to other pages to text boxes

At the moment, my Menu page is blank. So, what I want to do is add links to the individual course pages.

Double-click on a blank part on the webpage to bring up the circle edit menu. Then click on the TT icon to add a textbox.

From the toolbar, click on the Insert link icon.

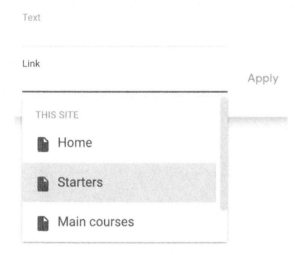

This opens a dialogue box and it needs two pieces of information. It needs the Text which will be visible on the page, and it needs the link.

In the link section, we can see the other pages we can connect to. Click on the page you want, in this case, Starters.

Text

Link

Apply

THIS SITE

📄 Home

📄 Starters

📄 Main courses

This updates the Text section automatically with the name of the page, although we could edit it if we wanted. Then click Apply.

This adds normal text which is underlined to show it's a link.

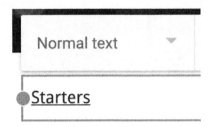

It's a bit small, so let's change it to a title using the drop-down menu in the toolbar.

The text box also covers the whole width of the page but as I want to add two other text boxes I need to reduce the size of it.

I click on the blue circle to the right of the text box and drag it to the left to make the textbox smaller.

If we click on the text, we will see the page it's linked to and we have the option to edit or delete it.

To add the other links, we could go through the same steps above, but to save having to format the text every time, I'm going to duplicate the section. Hover over the section, and select Duplicate section on the left-hand side.

This creates a copy of the section below the original one.

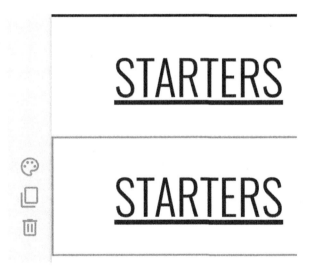

Next, we drag the copy to the section above by clicking on the text box when the crosshairs appear, near the top, middle of the textbox.

When we drag it into the other section, we see some guidelines appear to help us position it. Here I want the second textbox to be in the middle, so drop it as below.

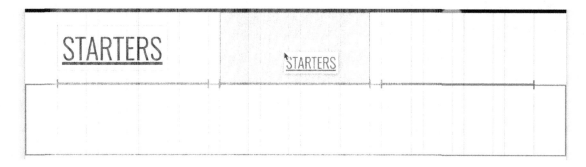

Next, we need to edit the text and link. Click on the text and then click the pencil icon to edit it.

It's currently linked to the Starters page.

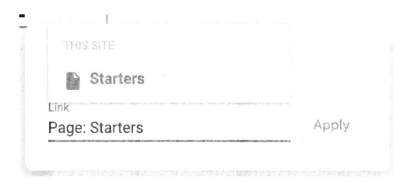

Delete the word Starters in the link and you will then see the other pages appear as options. Click on Main courses.

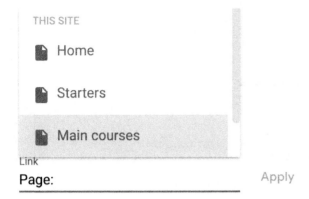

You will need to update the text too, as it isn't automatically updated. Then click Apply.

As the text is longer, drag the blue circle on the right-hand side a little to the right to make the text box longer.

Let's also centre the text within the box to make it easier to align on the page.

Let's do the same for the third course page. Duplicate the section.

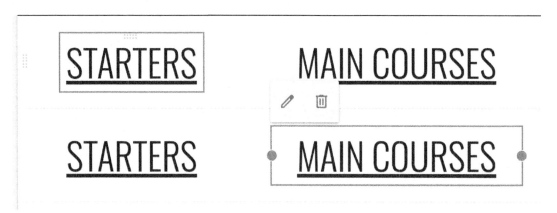

We don't need two text boxes, so let's delete the Main courses one. Click on it and select the Remove icon.

Click on it again and select the edit icon to link it to the Desserts page, as we did with the Main courses one.

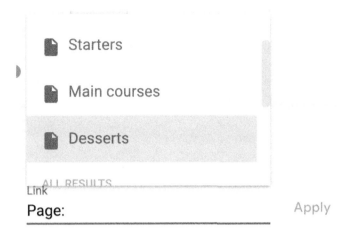

This leaves us with three text links to the three course pages. As you may notice, the three text boxes aren't aligned equally on the page.

So, all we do is move the Main courses one to the left a little and we end up with perfectly aligned textboxes.

Linking images and text to other pages

The above method is fine and works well, but most sites these days also have images linked to other pages in the site, which makes it look more modern and professional.

So, what we're going to do in this part, is add a layout with three images of the different courses and link both the images and the text below to the corresponding pages.

First, let's insert a 3-image layout.

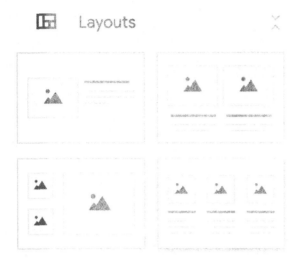

This is the same as we saw in an earlier chapter.

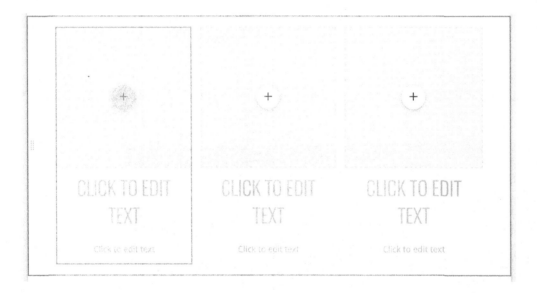

First, let's add the images. Click on the plus button and add images to each of the sections.

Here, we now have 3 images ready to be linked to the relevant pages.

To add a link to an image, click on the image and click the Insert link icon.

This will ask for the link you want to add. Click on the line under Link and select the page you want. Note, if it's an external link you can type in a URL here.

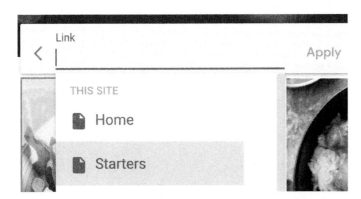

Here, I've selected the Starters page. Click Apply to add it.

Next, we don't need the second text boxes in each part.

Click on the text box and select Remove form the toolbar.

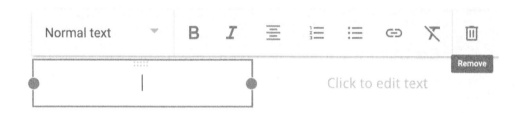

Adding a link to just the images is fine, but our customers might try to click on the text too thinking it will take them to the page. So it's best to also link the text under the images too.

Unfortunately, Sites as it stands, doesn't allow you to link the image and the text as one object, and then link to that one object. So, we'll have to add a link to the text separately.

Click on the Heading text below the image then select Insert link.

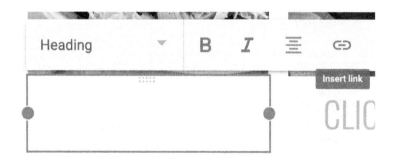

Select the page you want to link to.

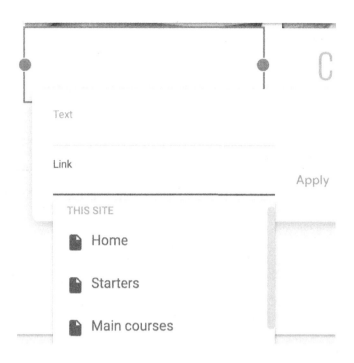

Then click Apply.

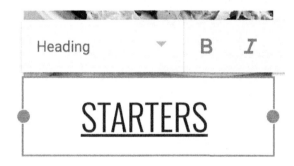

This adds the linked text below the image.

STARTERS

Here I've added the main courses and have shortened the text to Mains, so it fits better.

Text
Mains

Link
Page: Main courses   Apply

When we click on the textbox we can see which page it's linked to.

So, here's our Menu page with the links to the 3 separate course pages.

STARTERS   MAINS   DESSERTS

Inserting a page divider

The final thing I want to do on this page is add a page divider to show the end of the page better.

Go to the Insert menu and click on Divider.

Insert Pages

$\updownarrow$ Collapsible text

$\vdots\equiv$ Table of contents

$\blacksquare\square\blacksquare$ Image carousel

$\square$ Button

— Divider

This adds a divider to the page, which you can move around like any other of the page elements.

This looks like this:

9 – Adding a Google map

It's not just text and images we can add to our website, there are other types of elements we can include. Here, we're going to tell our customers where our bar restaurant is and include a mini Google map.

First, let's create a Find Us page. I want it on the same level as the homepage, so I click on the Home page in the Pages menu, then click the New page button.

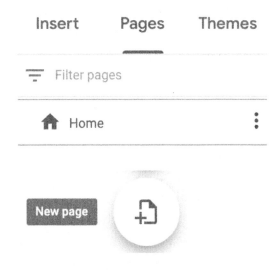

Enter the page name and click Done.

Then open the Insert menu and click on Map.

Insert   Pages

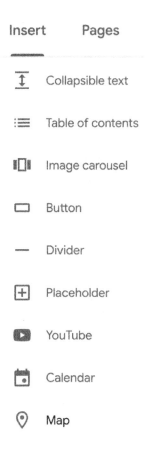

Collapsible text

Table of contents

Image carousel

Button

Divider

Placeholder

YouTube

Calendar

Map

This opens the map dialogue box where you need to enter a location.

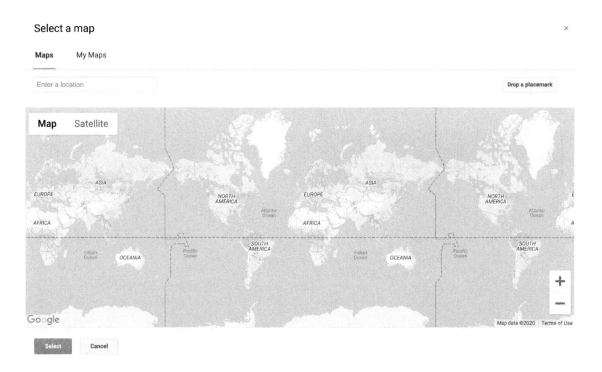

In the box where it says Enter a location, type in the address you want.

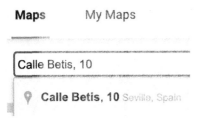

Then click on one of the options that appear. This will show the map of the area around that address and mark the address with a red marker. Click Select.

This will add the map to your webpage.

I want to add text to the left of the map, so I drag it over to the right.

We could also change the size of the map by dragging the blue circles, like we can with other elements.

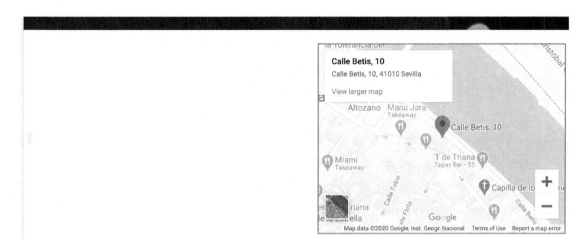

Now I add two text boxes. One for the sub heading "Where to find us" and the other for the address.

Where to find us

Baz's Bar & Restaurant

Calle Betis, 10

Seville

41001

Spain

So, very quickly we've created a Find us page.

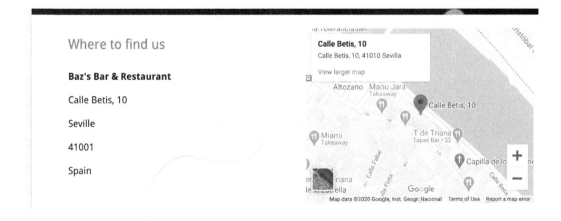

Let's just see what it looks like for the customer. Click on the Preview icon.

Preview

FIND US

Where to find us

Baz's Bar & Restaurant

Calle Betis, 10

Seville

41001

Spain

The map has a few options. Firstly, the user can click and drag it around.

Secondly, they can change the view of the map from the street map view to satellite imagery by clicking on the little square in the bottom left-hand corner.

They can also zoom in and out by clicking on the plus and minus buttons.

Finally, they can also open the map in a larger view by clicking on View larger map.

10 – Adding a calendar and a form

In this chapter, we're going to add a calendar to our site to show our customers what events are happening at our bar restaurant. Plus, we're going to add a Google Form to allow them to reserve a table.

Adding a calendar

First, let's create a new page called Events & reservations.

New page

Name

Events & reservations

Advanced ⌄   Done

Next let's add a calendar. From the Insert menu, click Calendar.

 Calendar

This will open a calendar dialogue box which will show you the calendars connected to your Google account.

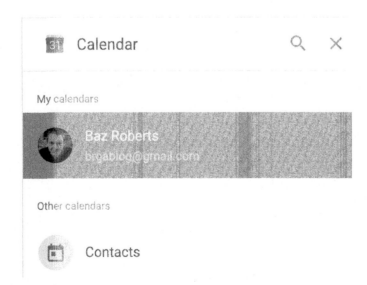

The first calendar is your default calendar and below that are other calendars that may be connected to your account. Here, I'm going to use the main calendar, so I click on the one with my name.

Click insert to add it (or just double-click on the calendar).

As you can see it's added the agenda view of the calendar. It's not the prettiest!

We can change the settings by clicking on the gear icon.

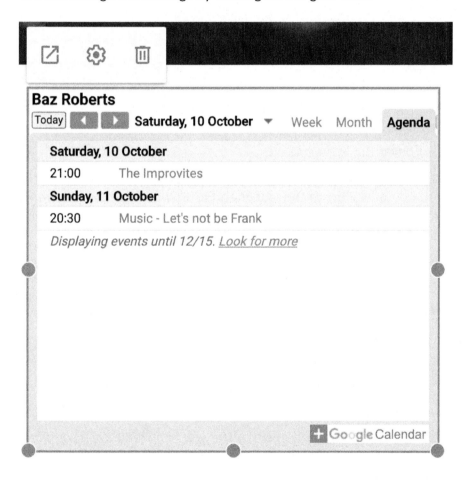

We can turn on or off the title, date, navigation buttons, time zone by toggling the switches. Here, I've turned the title of the calendar off and also the time zone.

Calendar Settings

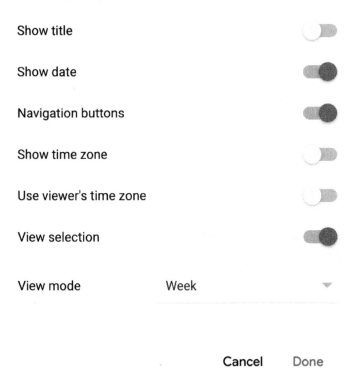

At the bottom, we can change the default view of the calendar. Either we can show the whole month, this week, or the agenda view. Here, I'm going to choose the Week view. View selection allows you to let the users change the calendar view or not.

Click Done to update the calendar. Now we can clearly see that this weekend we have a couple of events on.

Finally, I want the calendar to fill the page width, so I just drag the blue circles to the right.

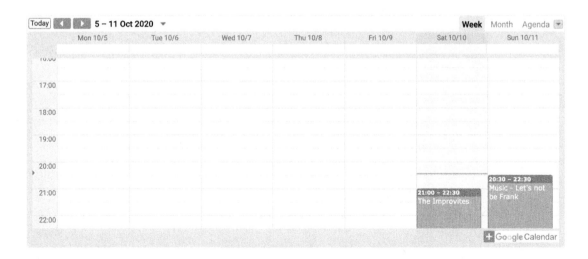

The nice thing is that when a customer clicks on an event, they get more information about it. Including the option to add it to their calendar.

Music - Let's not be Frank

When	Sun, 11 October, 20:30 – 22:30
Description	Local DJ spins some tunes

more details» copy to my calendar»

They can also navigate between weeks by clicking on the blue arrows at the top of the calendar.

Adding a reservation form

Next, let's add a form so that customers can make a reservation. First, we need to create a form on our Drive.

Open Drive and click the New button.

Then click Google Forms.

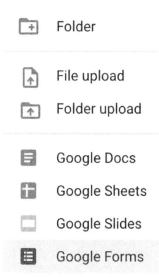

Folder

File upload

Folder upload

Google Docs

Google Sheets

Google Slides

Google Forms

If it's in a shared folder, click Create and share.

Create in a shared folder?   ✕

The created item will have the same sharing permissions as the selected folder.

CANCEL   CREATE AND SHARE

This will open a blank Google form.

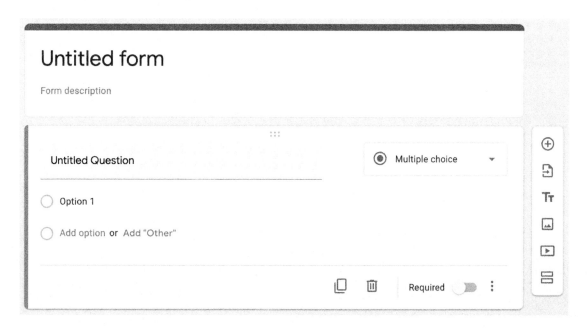

Next, give the form a title.

Reservations

Form description

Click on the filename and this should automatically change to your form title.

 Reservations

Click on the first question and type in Name.

Name

Short-answer text

Select "Short answer" from the question types.

 Short answer

 Paragraph

Make this question a required one.

Required

Then click the Add question plus button.

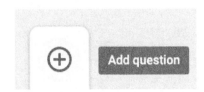

Add a date question. You will see the question type automatically changes when you type in Date.

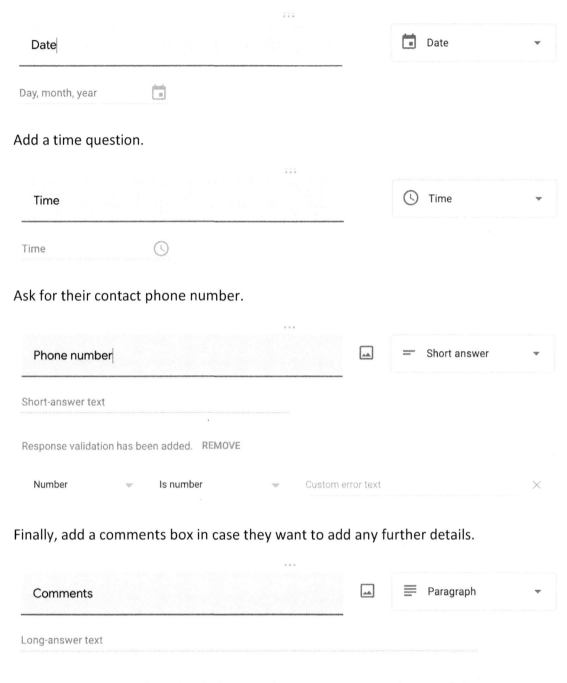

Date

Day, month, year 📅

Date ⌄

Add a time question.

Time

Time 🕐

Time ⌄

Ask for their contact phone number.

Phone number

Short-answer text

Short answer ⌄

Response validation has been added.   REMOVE

Number ⌄   Is number ⌄   Custom error text   ✕

Finally, add a comments box in case they want to add any further details.

Comments

Long-answer text

Paragraph ⌄

We can preview our form by clicking on the Preview icon at the top of the screen.

🎨 👁

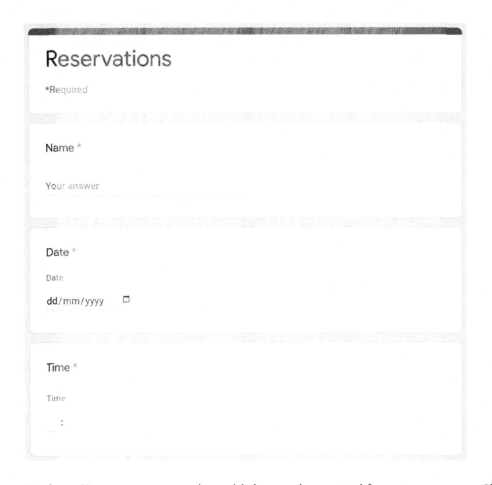

Back on Sites, we now need to add the newly-created form to our page. Click on the Insert menu.

Insert

Then click Forms.

Forms

This will open the Forms sidebar, where you look for your form and double-click on it to add it to the page.

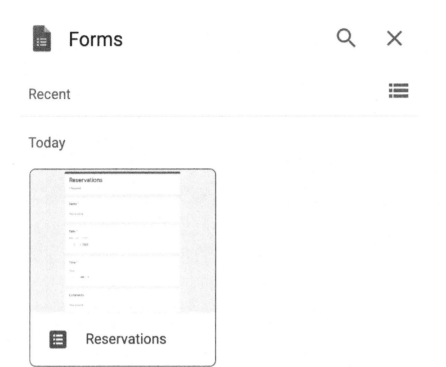

Here, I've centred the form on the page and also added a title. Plus, I've used Emphasis 1 to add a grey background to the title and the form.

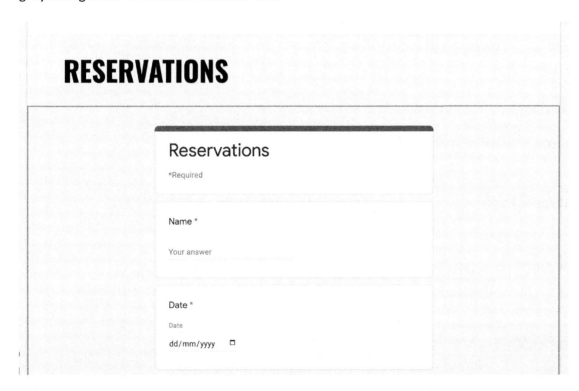

11 – Adding a video

A lot of sites these days contain videos and one of the easiest ways to add one is to upload it to YouTube and add a link to it on your site. In this chapter, we're going to add a video to our site from YouTube.

Adding a YouTube video

To add a video, click on the Insert menu and then YouTube.

Insert

 YouTube

This opens a dialogue box where you can search for the video or you can choose one from videos you've uploaded with your Google account.

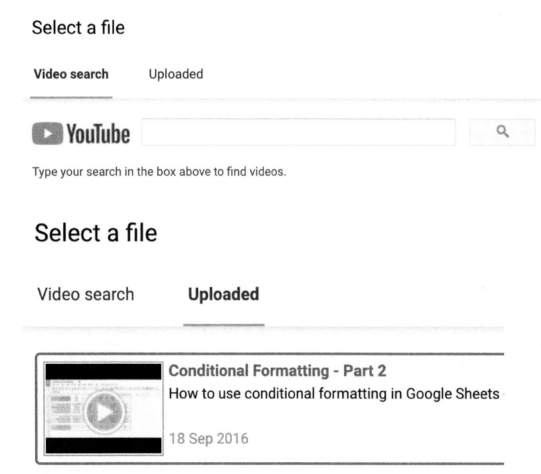

Select a file

Video search   Uploaded

YouTube [   ]   🔍

Type your search in the box above to find videos.

Select a file

Video search   **Uploaded**

Conditional Formatting - Part 2
How to use conditional formatting in Google Sheets

18 Sep 2016

As an example, I'm going to add a video of a restaurant opening event. Type in the search term and select a video from the videos that it finds.

Video search   Uploaded

 restaurant event

 **Restaurant Grand Opening Event**
Shoot for the launch event of the newest restaurant ir

5 min - 30 Aug 2018

Restaurant Review - FUMI Events | Atlanta Eats
Fumi is a restaurant that truly has it all: a gorgeous ar
sake selection, private dining, an all-out sushi bar and

59 sec - 2 May 2019

This adds the video to your page. It can be moved and resized like any other element you can add. There are also some settings you can change. Click on the gear icon to open the settings.

Here, you can change the controls and the progress bar, and allow it to be played in full screen or not.

101

YouTube video Settings

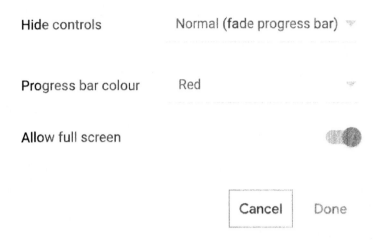

Hide controls   Normal (fade progress bar)

Progress bar colour   Red

Allow full screen

     Cancel   Done

The Hide controls has three options, basically do you hide the progress bar or not. Personally, I don't see much of a difference between the first two options.

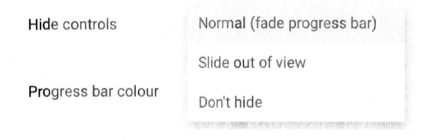

Hide controls   Normal (fade progress bar)

     Slide out of view

Progress bar colour   Don't hide

You can also change the colour of the progress bar.

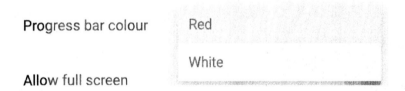

Progress bar colour   Red

     White

Allow full screen

Showing the preview of the site, we can see what the video looks like.

We can also see that you have the usual YouTube controls.

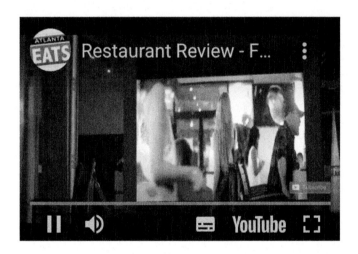

Finally, I'm going to centre the video and add a title and divider.

12 – Adding an image carousel

If we want to add lots of photos but don't want to take up much space on your webpage, you can use an image carousel, which shows an image one by one, either manually or automatically.

Adding an image carousel

I want to add some images taken from the opening event, and rather than display all the images individually on the page, we're going to make an image carousel.

Go to the Insert menu and click on Image carousel.

 Image carousel

This opens a dialogue box where you insert your images. Note, you need 2 or more images for the image carousel to work. Click on the plus button.

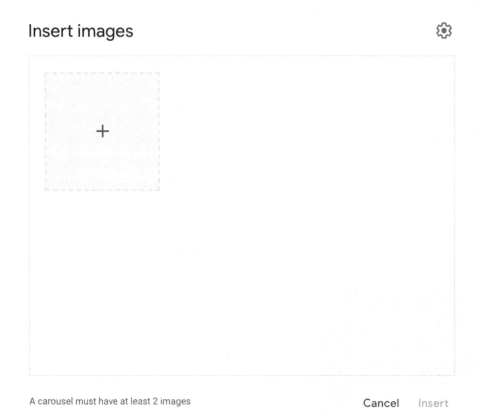

You can either upload images or select them from your Drive. I'm going to do the latter here. Click on Select image.

Upload image

Select image

Click on the images you want.

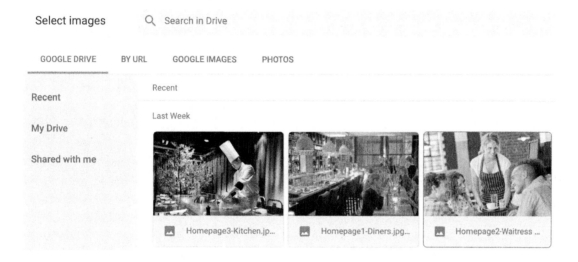

Then click Insert.

INSERT

As you can see this has added the images to the dialogue box.

Insert images

A carousel must have at least 2 images

Cancel   Insert

We also have a few options for our carousel. Click on the gear icon.

You can include dots to the carousel which show you which position the carousel is in. You can include captions the photos and also alt text for those who cannot see well. We'll look at this a little later.

We can also play the carousel automatically, which will share the images one-by-one for a few seconds.

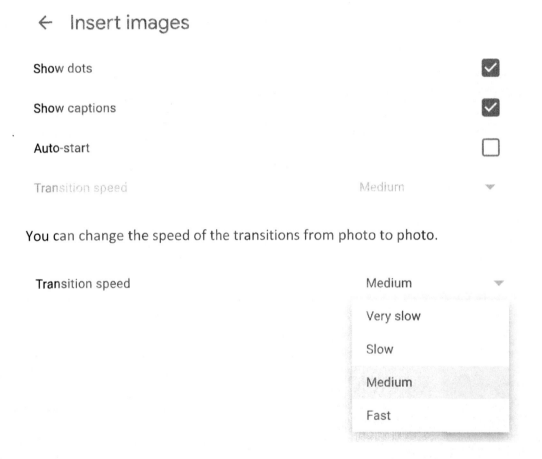

You can change the speed of the transitions from photo to photo.

As you can see it's added our carousel. As always we can move it and resize it.

Here's what it looks like in the preview mode.

Hovering over the carousel you will see navigation arrows appear allowing you to move through the photos.

Adding alt text to the carousel images.

In the Edit carousel dialogue box, if you hover over an image, you will have the option to either delete it or to add alt text or a caption. Click on the icon to the right.

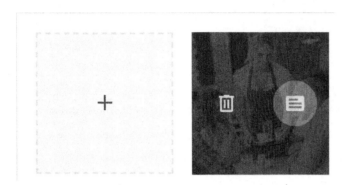

This shows you two options, to add alt text or a caption. Click on Add alt text.

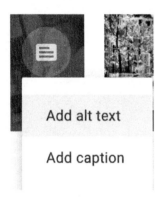

This opens the Alt text dialogue box.

Alt text

Alt text is accessed by screen readers for people who might have trouble seeing your content

> Description

CANCEL   APPLY

Type in the alt text you want and click Apply.

┌─ Description ────────────────────────────────────┐
│   │
│ Waitress serving customers| │
│   │
│   │
└───┘

CANCEL   APPLY

Adding a caption to an image

You can add captions to your images. In the Edit carousel dialogue box, hover over an image, click on the add caption icon and Add caption.

Add alt text

Add caption

This opens the Caption dialogue box. Type in the caption and click OK.

Caption

┌─ Description ────────────────────────────────┐
│   │
│ 5 star service| │
│   │
│   │
└──┘

Cancel   OK

Then click Update.

As you can see, we know have a caption to our photo.

5 star service

Here's what it looks like in the preview.

5 star service

13 – Adding collapsible text

In this chapter, we're going to look at adding collapsible text, which hides text in a drop-down menu, only showing it when the menu is clicked on.

This is great if you don't want to show lots of text on a page, and is also useful if you have different categories and you want to show the categories and not the details, unless someone clicks on them.

Adding collapsible text

From the Insert menu, click on Collapsible text.

↕   Collapsible text

Here, you add the that is visible as a menu, and below the text that is hidden unless it's clicked on.

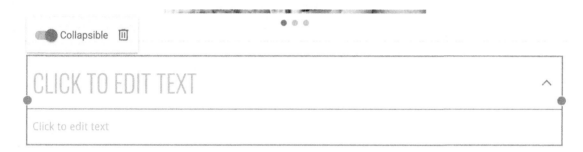

Here, I'm going to add the menu for the opening event.

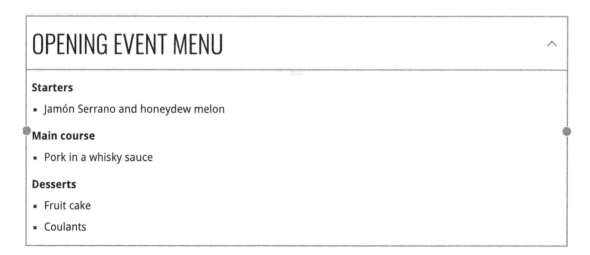

In edit mode it looks like this:

OPENING EVENT MENU	⌄

When we preview the site, we will see the menu with the text below not visible.

OPENING EVENT MENU ⌄

Clicking on the menu we will see the menu.

OPENING EVENT MENU ⌃

Starters

- Jamón Serrano and honeydew melon

Main course

- Pork in a whisky sauce

Desserts

- Fruit cake
- Coulants

Clicking on the element and turning the 'collapsible' toggle off, will convert it into a text box with a header and a normal text box below.

14 – Adding a footer

In this chapter, we're going to add a footer to the site with some basic details about the bar restaurant

This adds a footer to every page, but it is possible to delete it from certain pages. Hover over the bottom of the page and you will see the Add footer icon appear. Click on that.

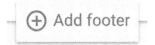

A text box will appear. Type in the text you want. By default the text is small, but you can change the text styling, add links, bullet points, etc, like you can with a normal text box.

In the preview mode it looks like this:

Notice the space it adds above the footer.

Hiding a footer from a page.

Hover over the footer and you will see the message "hide footer on this page". Click on the eye icon to hide the footer.

To show it again, click on the crossed-out eye icon.

15 – Publishing your website

Now the moment you've been waiting for, it's time to publish your website live on the internet so anyone can check it out. The great thing is that it's really easy and quick to do.

At the top-right of the site you have the blue Publish button. Click on that.

This will open a dialogue box, asking you to confirm the web address, who can access the site, and it you want it to be visible on search engines.

Publish to the web

Web address

> bazsbarandrestaurant

https://sites.google.com/view/**bazsbarandrestaurant**

Custom URL

Make it easier for people to visit your site with custom URLs such as www.yourdomain.co.uk   MANAGE

Who can view my site

Anyone MANAGE

Search settings

☐ Request public search engines not to display my site Learn more

Cancel   **Publish**

By default, the website URL is:

https://sites.google.com/view/ plus your specific site name. It uses the name we used for the site name. However, we can change it if we want and it will tell us if the name is available or not.

Web address

> bazsbarandrestaurant

https://sites.google.com/view/**bazsbarandrestaurant**

We have the choice of letting anyone view the site, or to restrict it to certain people or a particular domain. For this example, I want anyone to be able to view the site.

Who can view my site

Anyone MANAGE

If you want to change this, click on Manage. This will open the sharing dialogue box and show you who has can have access. Click on Change under the Links section.

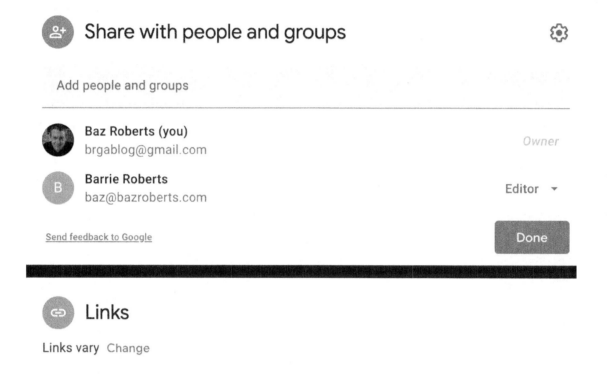

You can give one type of access to the edit mode (Draft) and another to the published site. Normally, you will want to restrict the Draft so that only certain people can edit the site.

Here, anyone can view the published site, but the draft is restricted.

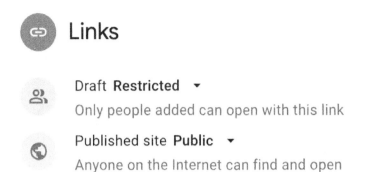

Links

Draft **Restricted** ▾
Only people added can open with this link

Published site **Public** ▾
Anyone on the Internet can find and open

To change it, click on the drop-down menus and select Restricted or Public, or remove the link completely.

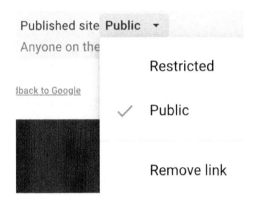

For more private sites, you can also choose to not have the site appear on search engines.

Search settings

☐ Request public search engines not to display my site   Learn more

Then click Publish.

Once published, the button in the top-right of the page will change and have a drop-down menu added to the Publish button.

Note, any changes you make to your site aren't visible until you republish your site.

More publishing options

Clicking on the drop-down menu of the Publish button, we can see Publish settings, a chance to review changes before publishing, view the published site, and a way of unpublishing it.

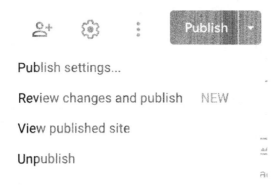

Publish settings

Click on Publish settings and we will see a dialogue box with similar options as the original Publish one. I.e. we can change the website address, use a custom URL, and not display the site on search engines.

For some reason the sharing options aren't on this menu and to change these you have to go to the Sharing menu, which we'll see in a later chapter.

Here, we have a new option. Any changes that are made to the site, we can add a review change before publishing the site. More information on this later.

Publish settings

Web address

bazsbarandrestaurant

https://sites.google.com/view/bazsbarandrestaurant

Custom URL

Make it easier for people to visit your site with custom URLs such as www.yourdomain.co.uk   MANAGE

Search settings

☐ Request public search engines not to display my site   Learn more

Review changes and publish

☑ Editors must review changes before publishing

Cancel   Save

Clicking on Review changes and publish at the moment shows that we have no unpublished changes, as we've just published the site.

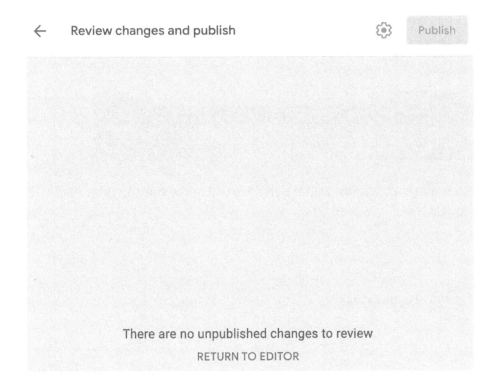

Clicking on View published site, we can see our live site:

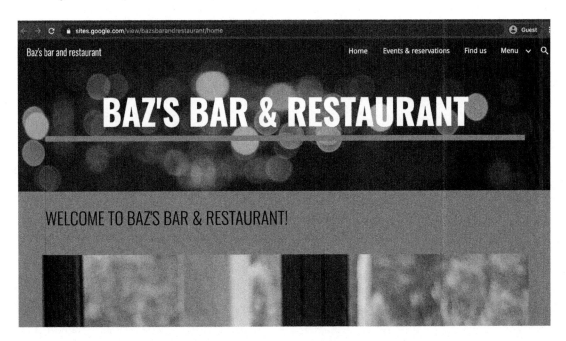

As you are an editor, you will notice that in the bottom right-hand corner there's an edit icon, which if clicked will take you to the edit site. This is only visible to you and not your customers.

There's also an I icon in the bottom left corner. Click on this. This shows when the page was last updated.

The final option in the Publish menu is to unpublish the site. This will make the site unavailable to the public. To do so, click Unpublish site and then OK.

Unpublish site

This site will no longer be live. You can still make edits and publish your site again.

Cancel   OK

Sharing published site link

Once a site is published, you can share specific page links.

To get the published link for a particular page whilst in edit mode, you can click on the link icon at the top of the page.

This will open a dialogue box where you can copy the link. Note, it's for the particular page you're currently on.

Published the site link   ✕

https://sites.google.com/view/bazsbarandrestaurant/home   Copy link

16 – Adding a Google Document

We're going to set up a new website for a language academy. This time it's going to be an internal one aimed at the teachers in that academy. It'll give us a chance to practise what we've already learnt and to learn even more things we can do with our sites.

In this chapter, after setting up the new site, we're going to add a Google Doc on the home page which will include important COVID information, which our teachers must read.

First, we create a new site, typing in the URL shortcut in Chrome, **sites.new**. This will create the new site and then we give it a name.

 Excellent English

Then we add 6 pages: Overview, Manuals, Teachers and a subpage for a teacher called Frank, Games, and News.

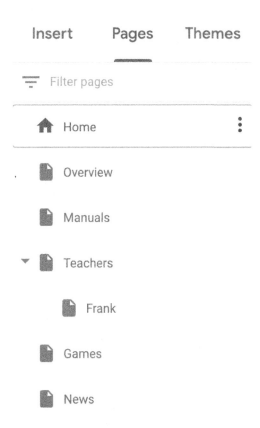

We're going to add the document to the homepage. First, change the page title to Home, and add a heading to welcome the staff.

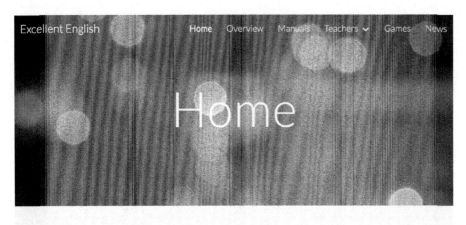

Welcome to the Excellent English internal website

Adding a Google Doc

Next, go to the Insert menu and click on Docs.

Insert

▤ Docs

This will open the Docs sidebar, where you then look for the Google Doc you need. As I've just created the COVID document it appears at the top.

▤ Docs

Recent

Today

Older

Double-click on it to add it. Here I've also added a text box asking the teachers to read the document. The good thing is that they can read the document right from within the page, but they also have the option of opening it in a new window.

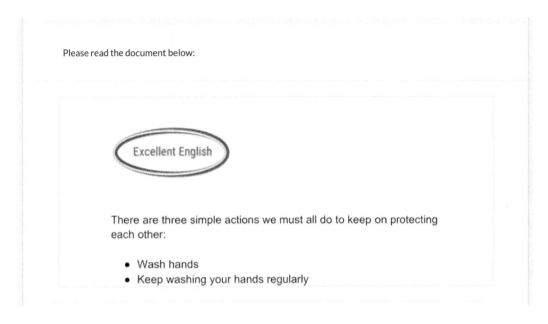

This is what it looks like in the preview. As you can see the user can scroll through the page.

17 – Adding a chart, slides, sheet, and table of contents

In this chapter, we're going to add a chart connected to a Google Sheet, a Slides presentation, a Google Sheet, and then link to all of them at the top of the page with a table of contents.

Open the page Overview. Here we're going to add information about the school and our future plans for it. I've added a heading.

Adding a chart from Sheets

Number of students

From the Insert menu, click on Charts.

Charts

This will open the Charts sidebar. Select the Google Sheet which contains your chart.

It will then prompt you to choose a chart that is within that Sheet. As I only have one chart, I select the first one and then click Add.

Select a chart

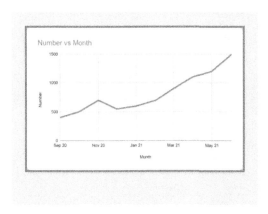

← Excellent English website stats

Cancel   Add

This adds the chart as an element to the page.

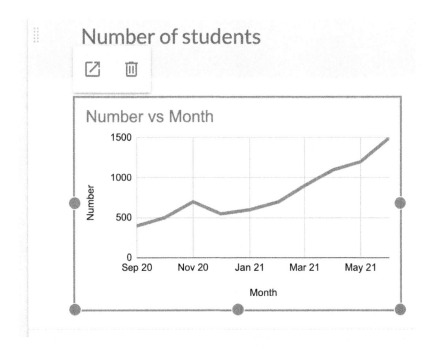

Here I've dragged it across and down to fill the page.

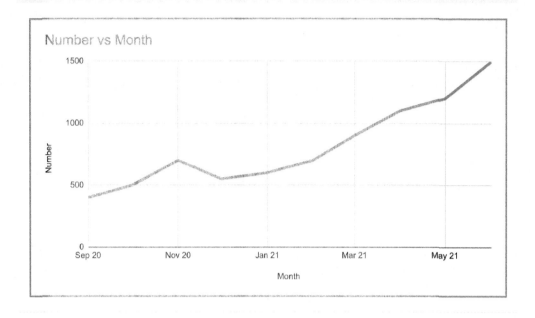

The good thing about adding charts is that the chart is dynamically connected to the original data, so if that is changed the chart is automatically updated.

As an example, I've changed the figures in the last month.

| 10 | May 21 | 1200 |
| 11 | Jun 21 | 200 |

As you can see, when I refresh the page, the chart has been updated.

Number of students

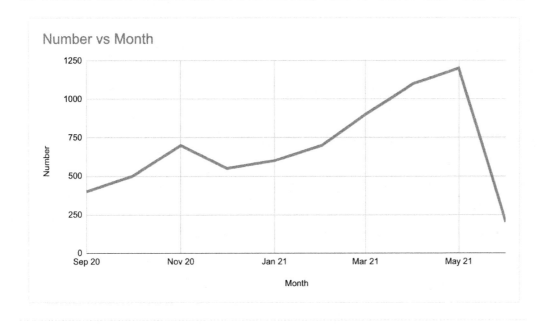

Adding a Slides presentation

Next, let's add a Slides presentation which will tell our teachers the upcoming plans we have. First, I add another header.

2020 Changes

Then go to the Insert menu and click Slides.

🔲   Slides

This will open the Slides sidebar. Find and double-click on the slides file you want.

Slides

Recent

Today

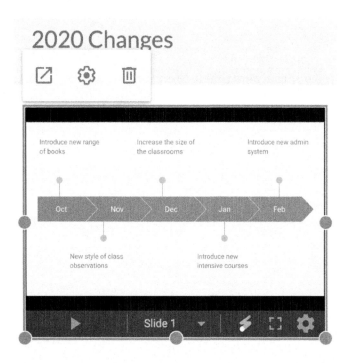

2020 plans

This will add the Slides as a presentation to your page. As with all elements, you can resize and reposition it.

When you hover over the element you can see there are settings you can edit. Click on the gear icon to open them.

Here you can auto start the presentation and set it to loop around, set the time per slide, and decide which slide to start it from.

Presentation Settings

Auto-start

Loop playback

Delay time   2 seconds

Starting Slide   1

Cancel   Done

Under Delay time, you have a few time settings to choose from.

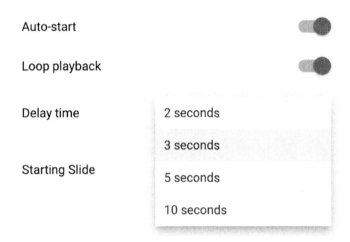

As my particular presentation only has one slide, I'm going to leave the Auto-start off.

Using the preview option, we can see what it will look like on the webpage:

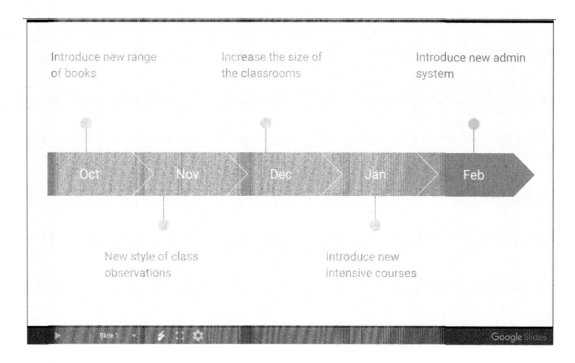

The viewer can play the presentation and select specific slides to go to from the toolbar at the bottom of the presentation.

If you make any changes to the slides, the presentation will automatically update when the page is refreshed. It's also a good way to share your presentation without giving access to the Slides file.

Adding a Google Sheet

Next, we're going to add a Google Sheet with an action plan. Go to the Insert menu and click on Sheets.

 Sheets

This will open the Sheets sidebar. Find the file you want and double-click it to add it to the page.

▥ Sheets

Recent

Today

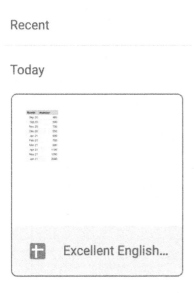

☩ Excellent English...

This particular file has 2 sheets and a chart, Students, StNumbs (chart), Actions. By default, it will show the first page first, but we can change that in the settings.

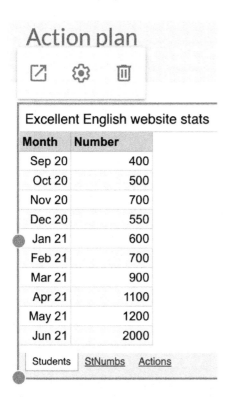

Hover over the element and click on the gear icon.

Excellent English we

From here, we can set which page is displayed first. Click on the drop-down menu.

Spreadsheet Settings

Sheet   Students   ▾

Cancel   Done

This will list the sheets in the file. Here I'm going to select the Actions sheet.

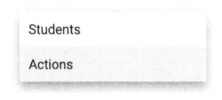

Then click Done.

Actions   ▾

Cancel   Done

Now we have the action plan page showing first.

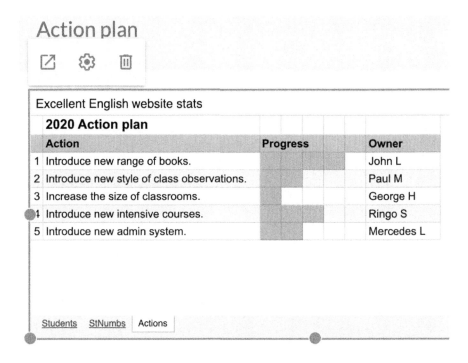

Action plan

Excellent English website stats		
2020 Action plan		
Action	**Progress**	**Owner**
1 Introduce new range of books.		John L
2 Introduce new style of class observations.		Paul M
3 Increase the size of classrooms.		George H
4 Introduce new intensive courses.		Ringo S
5 Introduce new admin system.		Mercedes L

Students   StNumbs   Actions

There are two important points to take into account when sharing a Google Sheet:

1) The user must have access to that sheet, so either specifically with their Google account or where it's open to anyone with a link.

If it's not shared, then the viewer will see this message:

 Google Sheets

We're sorry. This document is not published.

2) Website viewers will have access to all the sheets within that document, which you may or may not want to give.

To access the other sheets they just need to click on the tabs at the bottom of the page.

Adding a table of contents

Finally, as we have a few elements on our page, let's make it easy for the user to navigate to a specific part on the page. This is particularly useful for longer pages with various sections.

We can do this by adding a table of contents at the top of the page. This is basically an electronic version of the contents page of a book. It works by automatically grabbing the headers and sub-headers on the page and listing them all as links.

Go to the Insert menu and click on Table of contents.

≡≡ Table of contents

This will automatically add the element to the top of the page and fill it with the titles, headers, or sub-headers on the page.

Here it's added the 3 headers we created earlier. If there are sub-headers, they are indented from the left.

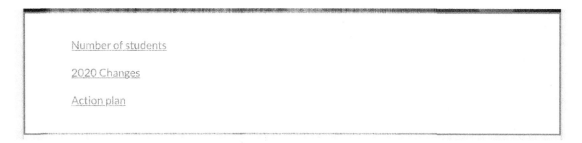

You also have the choice of hiding some of them. Hover over a link and you will see an eye icon. Click on it to hide that link.

To show it again, hover over the link and click on the crossed-out eye icon.

Number of students ⊘ Show

We can also style the background in the same way as text box, etc by clicking on the palette icon on the left. Here I've changed the background to Emphasis 2.

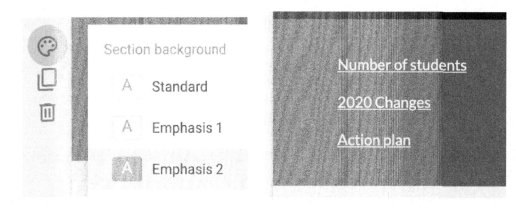

18 – Adding a placeholder

When we're building a website, we often want to build the overall structure of it first and that later go in and add the images, documents, etc. This allows us to lay out the pages and this is particularly helpful when we're working on a site together with others. The other people can clearly see the layout and what elements should be where.

To do this, we use placeholders, which can be set to accept certain types of files.

For this chapter, we're going to use the Manuals page, so first of all go to that page.

Go to the Insert menu and click on Placeholder.

[+]   Placeholder

This will add a placeholder element on the page. Click on the gear icon to edit the settings.

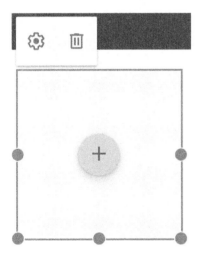

This will open a dialogue box where you can set the type of file for that element. Note, you don't have to do this, you can just leave it open but then a collaborator may not know what type of element you want to put here.

Click on the Any content drop-down menu.

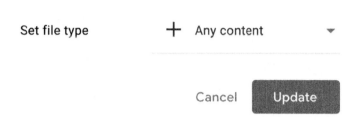

Placeholder settings

Site editors will be able to replace this with their own content

Set file type   ╋   Any content   ▼

Cancel   **Update**

As you can see, there is a nice range of elements you can set. In this example, I'm going to add a Google Doc, so I click on google Docs.

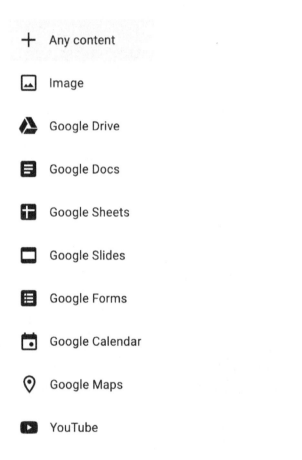

╋   Any content

▫   Image

▲   Google Drive

▤   Google Docs

▦   Google Sheets

▭   Google Slides

▤   Google Forms

▦   Google Calendar

⊙   Google Maps

▶   YouTube

Then click Update to add that file type to the placeholder.

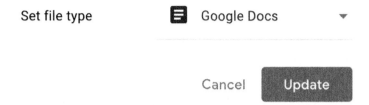

Set file type   📄   Google Docs   ▼

Cancel   **Update**

We can now see the icon in the middle of the placeholder has changed to a Google Doc icon, telling us that a Google Doc should be placed here.

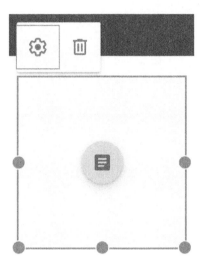

To add the Doc, click on the icon.

This opens the Docs sidebar. Find the document you want and double-click on it to add it.

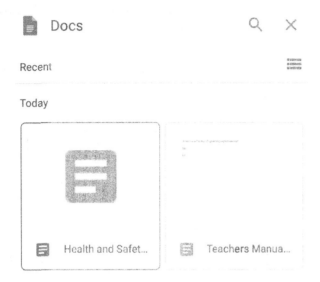

That will add the document in that element. It then turns that element into the element type you chosen, in this case a Google Doc element.

If we go to the page preview, we can see I've added two documents, along a couple of headers.

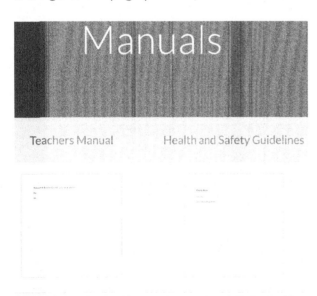

19 – Adding buttons

In this chapter, we're going to look at buttons which will allow us to easily link to other parts of the website or to open external links, for example, a Google form to do their attendance.

As an example, we're going to set up a page for one of our teachers, Frank, where they will have access to the attendance forms for two of the classes, and to be able to download a PDF version of the teacher manual by clicking on a button.

Adding buttons

To add a button, go to the Insert menu and click on Button.

▭   Button

This will open the Insert button dialogue box.

Insert button

Name
|

0/120

Link

Cancel   Insert

You need to enter 2 pieces of information, the name that will appear on the button, and the link it will go to when the user clicks on the button.

Here I'm setting up a button so the teacher can access the attendance form by clicking on a button on the page, straight from their phone, so I add the link to the Google Form. Then click Insert.

Insert button

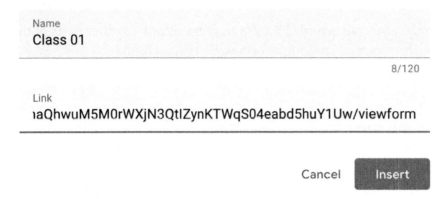

This will add the button on the page. By default, it uses a filled button, which is one which is filled with the theme colour.

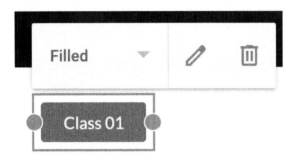

There are 3 button styles: Filed, Outlined, and just plain Text.

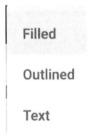

The Outlined one is without a coloured background.

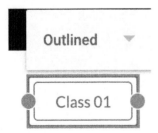

The Text one is just the words and is a clickable link.

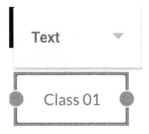

Clicking on the pencil icon, allows you to edit the name or the link connected to the button.

Edit button

Name
Class 01

8/120

Link
https://docs.google.com/forms/d/e/1FAIpQLSfReUKfAJnaQ...

Cancel   Update

Adding a button to download a PDF of a Google Doc

Next I'm going to add another button where when the teacher clicks on it, it will download a PDF of the Teachers Manual.

The document is on my Drive as a Google Doc and first I get the link to that and paste it in. Then I replace the last part of the URL **/edit** with **/export?format=pdf**

Gy34/export?format=pdf

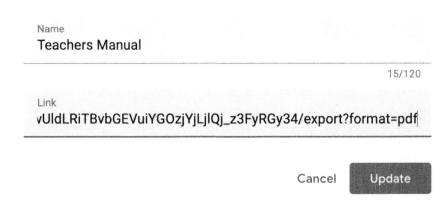

Edit button

Name
Teachers Manual

15/120

Link
vUldLRiTBvbGEVuiYGOzjYjLjlQj_z3FyRGy34/export?format=pdf

Cancel   Update

When the link opens it will open a new page and then download the Google Doc as a PDF automatically.

Apart from making it easy to download a PDF from your Drive, it also means you don't have to store the PDF on the Drive, this saving space and allowing you to still be able to edit the Google Doc.

Open the preview of the page, we can see the two buttons we've created.

Clicking on the first one opens the attendance form, where the teacher can easily enter their attendance on the Google Form.

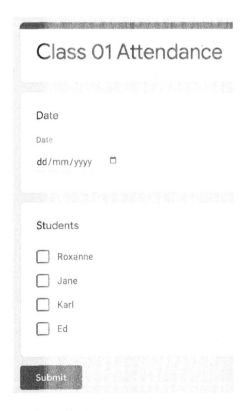

Clicking on the second, downloads the PDF in the browser.

Duplicating a button

If you want to make other similar buttons I find it easier to duplicate the section where the button is. Click on the Duplicate section icon on the left-hand side.

As you can see it makes an identical copy below the original, so you don't have to style it again.

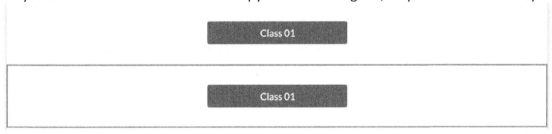

If you want to add the second button on the original row.

Drag it to the section above.

Resizing a button

It's easy to change the size of the button, or at least the width of it. Just click on the button and drag one of the blue circles.

One thing you can't do is change the height of the buttons.

Changing the colour of the buttons

You can't individually change the colour of the buttons. The only way is to change the colour globally in the theme.

Go to Themes on the sidebar, click on the theme and select a colour.

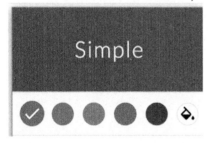

Here I'm changing it to pink.

This changes the colours of all the buttons.

Here's what the page looks like on the teacher's mobile (using the preview option and selecting the mobile view). As you can see it stacks the buttons in one column.

Class 01

Class 02

Teachers Manual

Linking to an internal webpage

Above we linked to files on my Drive but we can also link to external website, just by pasting in the URL, or we can link to a page within our website.

To do the latter, tap on the Link field in Edit button and you will see a list of the pages in your site. Just click on the page you want then click Update.

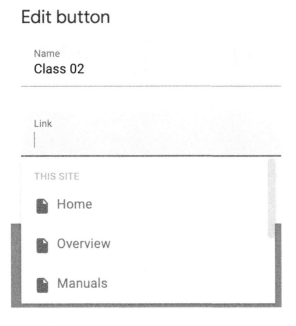

20 – Embedding code & games into a page

Web pages are made of code and the tools on Sites are a user-friendly way to create a site without having to worry about writing code to do it. All that happens in the background.

So far we've been adding elements that are built into Google Sites, but Sites also has the facility to add our own code to a page, which opens a whole world of possibilities, allowing us to add extra elements.

In this chapter, we're going to add some games to the Games page in three different ways, but what they have in common is that we're embedding code into the page.

Adding a revision game from a website

In the first example, we're going to embed a vocabulary matching game from the flashcard website Quizlet.com. When you make flashcards on the site, it also converts them into different games, allowing students to revise in different ways.

We're going to add this matching game to the Games web page.

On the set of vocabulary under the flashcards, there is a 3-dot menu.

NEF Upper-Int – File 3 – Weather

STUDY

- Flashcards
- Learn
- Write
- Spell
- Test

Play

- Match
- Gravity

Hace fresco (agradable).

Click again to see the term

1/50

Created by
barrieroberts

Click on that and you will see the option to embed. Click on Embed.

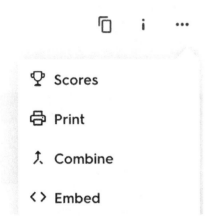

- Scores
- Print
- Combine
- <> Embed

You will see some HTML code in the box. You have a drop-down menu to select the type of game you want, in this case Match. Click on Copy HTML. This will copy the code in the box.

The beauty of this is that you don't need to understand any code, you just copy and paste it.

Embed study modes

Select a study mode from the drop down list, then copy and paste the HTML text to embed this set in your website or blog.

| Match ∨ | Copy HTML |

```
<iframe src="https://quizlet.com/33659214/match/embed?x=1jj1" height="500" width="100%" style="border:0"></iframe>
```

CODE TO BE EMBEDDED

Back on your site, click the Insert menu and Embed.

Insert

TT
Text box

< >
Embed

Or alternatively, double-click on a blank space on the page and then click Embed from the circle menu.

This will open Embed from the web dialogue box. There are two options:

1) Paste in a URL that connects to the code
2) Paste in the code directly in the box.

In this first example, we're going to paste in the code we just copied form the Quizlet website.

Click on Embed code.

Embed from the web

By URL   Embed code

```
<html> code goes here
```

Paste the HTML code from the site that you want to embed.

Cancel   Next

Then paste in the code in the box and click Next.

Embed from the web

By URL   Embed code

```
<iframe src="https://quizlet.com/33659214/match/embed?x=1jj1"
height="500" width="100%" style="border:0"></iframe>
```

Paste the HTML code from the site that you want to embed.

Cancel   Next

A preview of the content will appear. If there are any problems it will show an error here. If it all looks ok, click Insert.

Embed from the web

By URL   Embed code

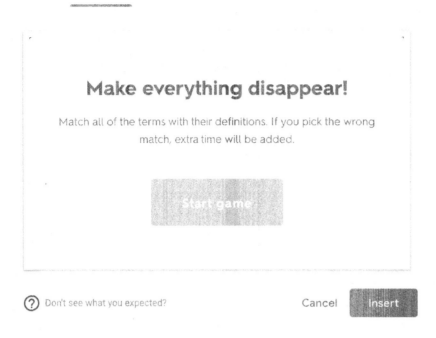

? Don't see what you expected?   Cancel   Insert

As we can see it's added the intro to the game on our webpage.

We can test it out by clicking on preview.

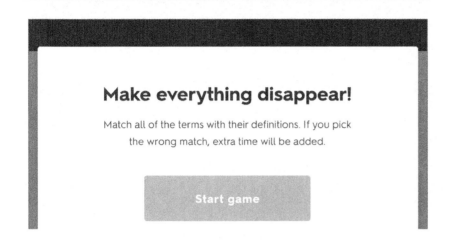

Then click Start game and the game will start right on our webpage.

This means that our students don't have to go to another website they can access it without leaving this one. It also allows us to organise the games on the page and we want and to choose just the ones we want.

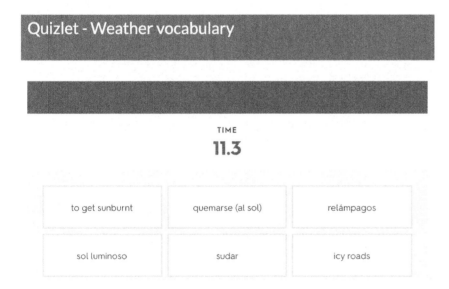

Adding a game written in Apps Script

In this next example, we're going to add a simple card game I wrote. Behind a number of the Google Apps there is the option to write code to automate things and in this case to make a card game webpage. It uses a programming language which is a variant of JavaScript called Google Apps Script.

Ladder Game

We'll email you the (final) _____.

We're _____ to...

The _____ is to...

The cards in the game are stored in a Google Sheet. When the link is opened the program grabs these cells and creates the webpage with the cards on it.

	A	B
1	**Questions**	**Answers**
2	We'll email you the (final) _____.	We'll email you the (final) ITINERARY.
3	We're _____ to...	We're PLANNING to...
4	The _____ is to...	The IDEA is to...

You don't need to know how all this works, but it's an example of how we can add code via a URL. If you'd like to know more, check out my blog post on it here:

https://www.bazroberts.com/2020/05/03/ladder-card-game-using-google-sheets/

In Sites, click on Insert and Embed.

Embed from the web

By URL   Embed code

_____

```
┌─────────────────────────────────────────────────────┐
│                                                       │
│                                                       │
│                                                       │
└─────────────────────────────────────────────────────┘
```
Enter URL

Cancel   Insert

In the By URL section, paste in the webpage link.

https://script.google.com/macros/s/AKfycbxuxEdbnF3GxR5stxPFusryeoAfEAd-FBEa3jyT/exec

Underneath you will see a preview of the page appear. Click Insert.

Embed from the web

By URL   Embed code

_____

```
┌─────────────────────────────────────────────────────┐
│  cros/s/AKfycbxuxEdbnF3GxR5stxPFusryeoAfEAd-FBEa3jyT/exec │
└─────────────────────────────────────────────────────┘
```
Enter URL

Cancel   **Insert**

This has now embedded the card game on the webpage.

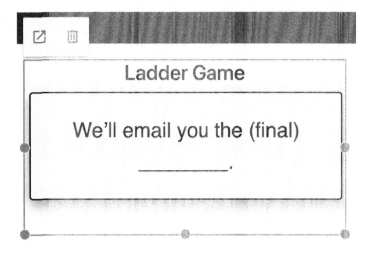

In the preview, we can check that it's all working ok.

Ladder Game

We'll email you the (final) _____.

We're _____ to...

Like the previous example, it's great that they can do this right from within the same website.

Embedding elements as a full page

You can also embed elements as a full page, rather than having multiple elements on a page.

From Pages, click "Full page embed".

It will create a new page, so you will need to give it a unique name.

New full page embed

Name

Game

Advanced ▾   Done

You then have the choice of embedding an element via a URL or code, or you can add a file form your Drive.

Embed a file, map or video from the Insert sidebar. You can also
write custom code. The content will fill the page.

| Add embed | Add from Drive |

Here I'm going to add a form from my drive. I just find the file, select it, and click "Insert".

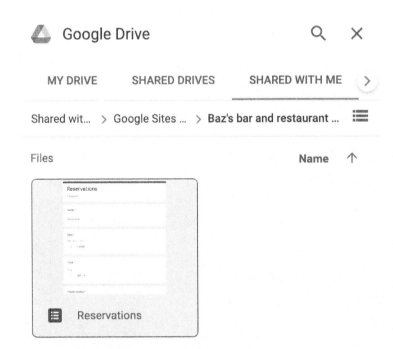

This will create a new page and add the form to it, so that it takes up the whole page.

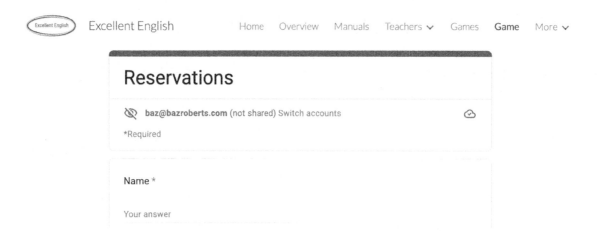

You can also embed code either via a URL or paste in the code, similar to what we saw earlier in this chapter.

Embed from the web

By URL   Embed code

```
<iframe src="https://quizlet.com/33659214/match/embed?x=1jj1"
height="500" width="100%" style="border:0"></iframe>
```

Paste the HTML code from the site that you want to embed.

Cancel   Next

The difference is that it creates a new page and fills that page with the element.

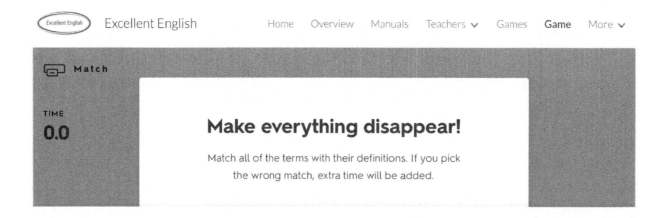

21 – Adding an announcement banner

Another feature you often see on websites is a temporary message in the form of a banner, which announces something to the viewer. Sites has this facility too and we're going to use it to announce some new news to our teachers.

First of all, we need to add some news to the News webpage. Here I've just added two pieces of news using text boxes.

Next we need to add the announcement banner. At the top of the page, click on Settings.

The Settings dialogue box will open. Click on Announcement banner.

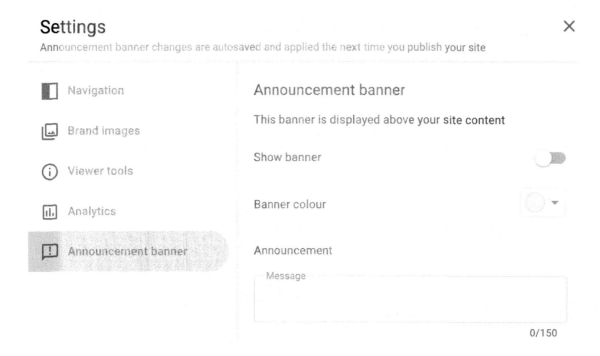

To turn the announcement on or off, toggle the option Show banner. Underneath, you have a drop-down where you can select from a range of colours.

Announcement banner

This banner is displayed above your site content

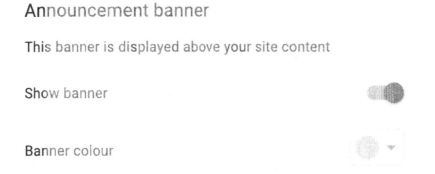

Next, add the message you want to display on the banner.

You can add a button to the banner, which will take them to a new page. This is optional but as I want to take them to the News page, I've added a Click here message to the button.

Announcement

Message

New! - Induction

16/150

Button label

Click here

10/25

Underneath, click on the Link box and select the News page.

Finally, you have the option to open the page in a new tab when they click the button, and also to display the banner on all the pages or just on the Home page.

☐ Open in new tab

Visibility   ○ Home page only

                   ◉ All pages

Close the dialogue box by clicking on the X.

If necessary, refresh the page and you will see the banner at the top of the page. Clicking on the button will take them to the News page.

We can also see that on the teacher's page, we still see the banner, so that the teachers will always see the latest news when they are using their webpage to do their attendance, etc.

To turn the banner off, just go back to Settings and toggle the Show banner option.

22 – Adding links to the menu

As we've seen in an earlier chapter, when we create a new page it adds it automatically to the navigation bar. However, we can add other links to that too.

In this chapter, we're going to add a link to my website, so that my teachers can learn how to use the Google apps better.

To do this, we need to go to the Pages menu on the sidebar.

Pages

Then at the bottom, hover over the plus button. Apart from adding a page you will also see the option to add a new link. Click on that button.

This will open the New link dialogue box. Here you will need to name the link and provide a URL.

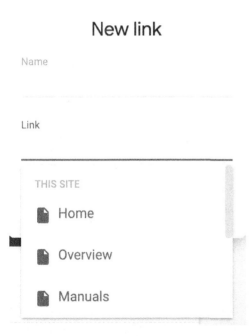

New link

Name

Link

THIS SITE

Home

Overview

Manuals

Here I'm going to call it Training and add the link to my site. We also have the option for it to open in a new tab when clicked on. Then click Done.

New link

Name

Training

Link

www.bazroberts.com

☑ Open in new tab

Done

This adds the link on the Pages menu, similar to adding a page. You can move it to a different position if you like. Just click on it and drag it to a new position.

 Home

Training

Here, I've moved it to the bottom of the pages, so it's last on the list.

 News

Training

Clicking on the 3-dot menu to the side of the link, brings up the options to rename it or change the link, hide it from the navigation, or to delete it.

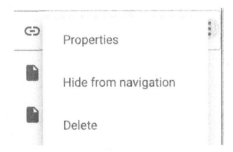

Properties

Hide from navigation

Delete

As you can see it's added it to the navigation bar too.

News   Training

Adding a new menu section

We can also add a menu section to the menu, which allows us to add pages under it without the need to create a page.

Go to Pages and click "New menu section".

Give the section a name.

New menu section

Name

Examples

Done

This will add the section in the Pages sidebar. I can then drag and drop a page onto it, to then link that page to that section.

We can then see the new menu section on the menu with the Games page under it.

23 – Controlling access to a site

Our English academy site is ready to publish. In a previous chapter, we looked at publishing a site but we wanted to allow anyone have access to the site, whereas here we only want it available to certain people in our organisation. So, we're going to look at how we restrict access both to the draft site where we edit it and to the published site.

To publish the site click the Publish button.

This will open the Publish to the web dialogue box. Type in the name of your site. Then click Manage under Who can view my site.

Publish to the web

Web address

excellentenglishacademy ⊘

https://sites.google.com/view/**excellentenglishacademy**

Who can view my site

Anyone MANAGE

Search settings

☐ Request public search engines not to display my site <u>Learn more</u>

This will open the sharing options. As you can see at the moment, it's shared with my bazroberts account and I have editor access with that account.

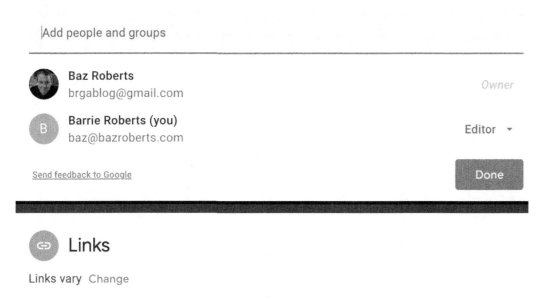

Links

Links vary Change

Under Links click on Change.

Links

Links vary Change

Here we have two options, one for the Draft site – the one we edit, and one for the published site. At the moment, only certain people can edit it, but the whole world can view it.

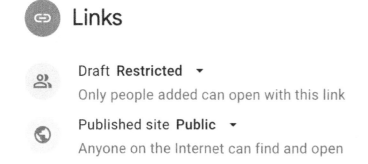

Links

Draft **Restricted** ▾
Only people added can open with this link

Published site **Public** ▾
Anyone on the Internet can find and open

Click on Public in the second option and you will see that you can restrict the access to the published site. Click on Restricted.

Restricted

✓ Public

Remove link

Now we have restricted access to both the draft and published site. Click Done.

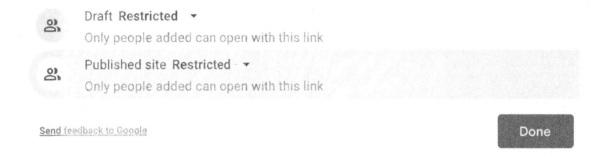

Draft **Restricted** ▾
Only people added can open with this link

Published site **Restricted** ▾
Only people added can open with this link

Send feedback to Google

Done

Giving view rights to a user but not edit rights

We can also give just view rights to a site and not full edit rights. Click on the Sharing icon at the top of the screen.

In the first part with the list of people who have access, you will see that Barrie Roberts has editing rights at the moment. Click on Editor.

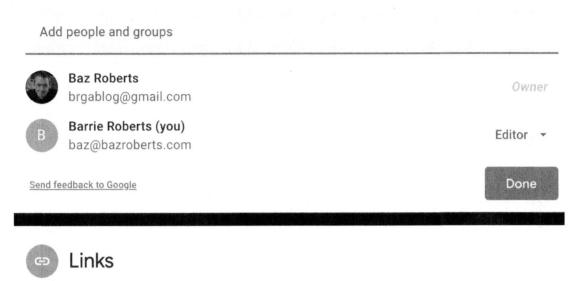

Click on the option Published Viewer which will give him only viewing rights to the published site, and he won't be able to edit the Draft site.

Then click Save.

| Published Viewer ▾ |

Pending changes Save

Incidentally, this is where you can remove a user too, by clicking on Remove, and where you can change the owner of the site, by clicking on Make owner.

When Barrie Roberts tries to open the Draft site now, they will see this 404 error page.

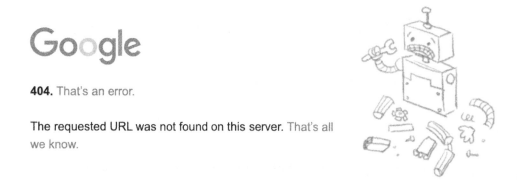

More sharing options in Drive

In Drive, if we right click on the site file, we can access the sharing options as we would any other file in Drive. Click Share.

In the top right corner, click on the cog icon to open settings.

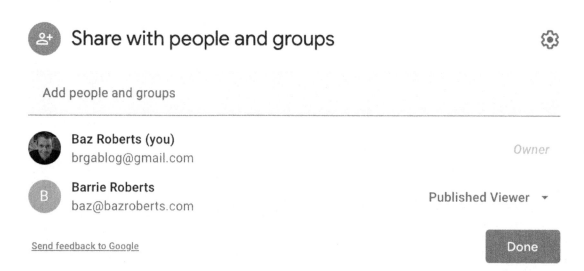

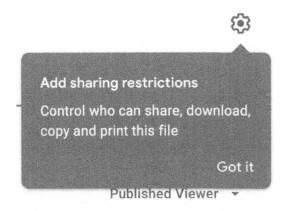

Here we can control whether we want to allow someone to be able to publish, change permissions, and add new people. Untick it if you don't want them to be able to do this.

← Share with people settings

☑ Editors can publish, change permissions and add new people

Sharing the draft site with anyone with a link

We have two options when sharing the Draft site, one with specific people as we've done above, but we can also share it with anyone with a link.

To do so, in the sharing box, click on Restricted next to Draft. Then select Anyone with a link.

🔗 Links

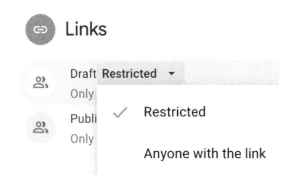

Note, when they click on the link they will need to log in with their Google account. So, you will still be able to see who has made any changes.

Sharing with a domain

If you have a Google Workspace account or an Education one, you can also share a site with anyone within that domain.

Here I've got a domain called bazroberts, so I just click on that and **anyone within that domain can have** access to it.

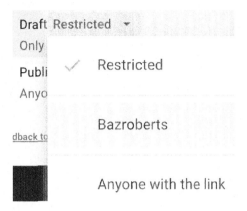

Reviewing changes to your site before publishing

Here, I've made a little change to my site and I'm going to republish it. I click on Publish again and this time it asks me to review the changes I've made before publishing to the world. This is particularly useful if you have multiple people editing the site.

Once everything is OK, click Publish.

You can turn this option off by clicking on the cog icon in the above screen.

Then unticking Editors must review changes before publishing.

Publish settings

Web address

excellentenglishacademy

https://sites.google.com/view/**excellentenglishacadem**

Custom URL

Make it easier for people to visit your site with custor

Review changes and publish

☑ Editors must review changes before publishing

You can also access this by clicking on the little triangle next to Publish and selecting Publish settings.

Publish settings...

24 – Version history

We've now finished with creating the two example sites in this book and it's time to look at some of the other tools in Sites.

In this chapter, we're going have a quick look at the Version history. This is a record of every change you do to the site. This means that you can always correct any mistakes, you can go back to previous version, and also see who did what if you've shared the site for editing.

To access it, go to the 3-dot menu at the top right of the page and click on Version history.

If you've used Version history in Google Docs, Sheets, etc this will be very familiar. On the left you have your page and the right a sidebar with the different versions of the site ordered by date and time.

Clicking on a date will bring up the site as it was at that time. By default it shows you the main changes, but if you click on the little triangle to the left of the date, it will show you smaller changes which you can select if you are looking for specific ones.

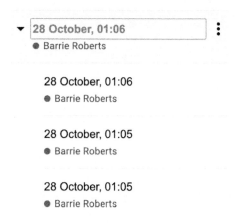

Restoring a revision

To go to that revision, click on the date.

MONDAY

▶ **26 October, 10:49**
  ● Barrie Roberts

For example, I have since added collapsible text to the News page but here's before I did that and it shows the original text boxes.

████████████████████████████████

28th Sep - Induction meet up in the patio at 12:00 on Friday, 2nd Oct.

21st Sep - Books are ready to be collected from reception.

Then in the top left of the screen, you will see the option to restore this version. Click on that to do just that. You can click on the arrow to navigate out of the Version history page.

← 26 October, 10:49   **Restore this version**

Naming a revision

We can name revisions which is useful if we want to highlight specific moments, for example, maybe the first release of this website to the teachers, would be revision 1. To do so, click on the 3-dot menu next to the revision date you want. Then click Name this version.

Here I've called it Revision 1.

▶ **Revision 1**

Current version

● Barrie Roberts

The good thing about naming versions, is so that you can filter the number of versions to a select few and to communicate to others what revisions happened when, so they are easy to find.

One useful little tool, is to show only the named versions. On the sidebar, toggle Only show named versions on.

Only show named versions

This will then only list the ones that have been named.

Only show named versions

TODAY

Revision 1

28 October, 10:15

● Baz Roberts
● Barrie Roberts

You will also notice that it shows you who edited that particularly revision, by showing the editors.

25 – Duplicating a site

Sometimes you may want to make a copy of an existing site, for example, to use a master to make a similar new one or to back up the existing one. Sites makes it really easy to do.

In this chapter, we're going to duplicate our site from within Sites and also see how it's done in Drive.

Go to the 3-dot menu in the top right of the screen and select Duplicate site.

Version history

Duplicate site

This opens a dialogue box where you can rename the copy, change the folder location where it lives, and decide if you're going to share with the same editors or not. Then click Duplicate.

Duplicate site

File name

Copy of Excellent English

Folder

📁 Teachers - Internal site Change

Copy will be created in a shared folder.

Sharing

☐ Share with the same editors

Any change that you make to your site after starting a copy will not be reflected on the duplicate site.

Cancel   Duplicate

You will see this message appear at the bottom of the screen. For a small site like what we've created here, the process only takes a few seconds.

Copy started. Check your emails for updates. ✕

Open Drive and you will see a copy has been made in the folder you selected.

⊞   Copy of Excellent English

You can also make a copy right from within Drive just by right-clicking on the Site file and choosing Make a copy.

⎘   Make a copy

Note, this doesn't open the dialogue box as before, but you can easily change the name, move the Site file to a different location and change the sharing options.

26 – Further settings

In this chapter, we're going to look at the other options available to us in the Settings menu. These include:

-changing the position and colour of the navigation bar
-adding site logos and a favicon
-adding a brand colour to the site
-adding a last updated info icon
-adding Google analytics

Navigation bar options

Click on the cog icon to open the Settings menu.

Click on Navigation and you will see two options, Mode and Colour.

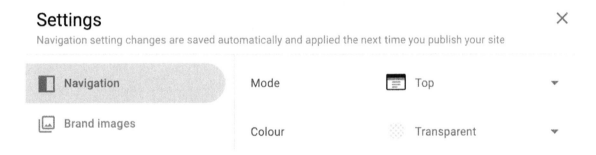

We can change the navigation from being at the top of the page, as it has been so far, to a menu on the side. Click Side.

This puts the menu in a 'hamburger' menu (3 lines icon).

Click on the hamburger menu and you will see the pages menu.

We can also change the colour of the menu. By default it's transparent but we can change it to a white or black background.

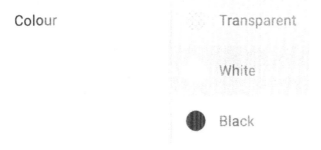

Here I've changed it to white.

Adding a logo

We can add a logo to our site which will appear in the top left-hand corner of every page next to the site title.

Click on Brand images, then under Logo, upload or select an image from your Drive.

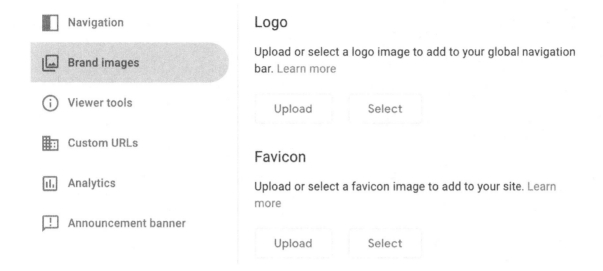

You have the option of adding Alt text.

Logo

Upload or select a logo image to add to your global
navigation bar. Learn more

> Alt text

Alt text is accessed by screen readers for people who might have
trouble seeing your content

Select a colour to use for theme

Plus you can match the colour scheme of your site to the colours in your logo. Click on one of the
colours it presents to you.

It's changed the theme colour to the blue colour (on the right) and changed for example, the button
colours.

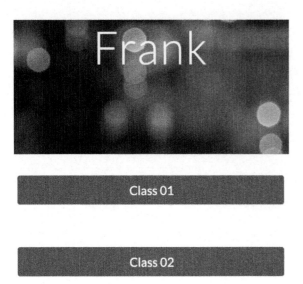

Class 01

Class 02

Adding a favicon

Under Brand images you can also add a favicon, which is a little icon that appears on your browser tab next to the site name. By default, it's the Google Sites logo but you can add your own.

Under Favicon, upload your icon image.

Favicon

Upload or select a favicon image
more

Upload   Select

Favicon

Upload or select a favicon image to ad
more

Excellent English

As you can see on the Chrome browser tab, it displays the icon.

Excellent English

Adding page last updated info

We can let our users know when a page was last updated. Click on Viewers tools and under Info icon, make sure the Show page last updated time is turned on, by default it is.

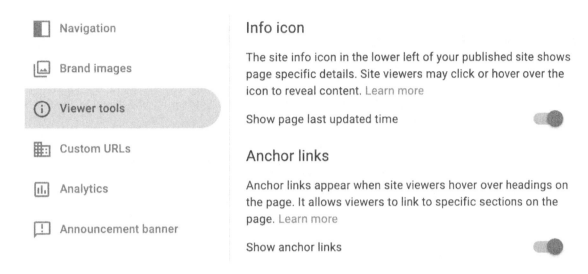

On the published site, you will see a little (i) icon in the bottom left-hand corner and when you click on that, you will see when that page was last updated.

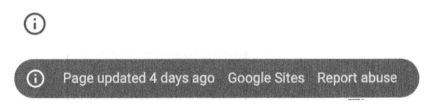

Linking to specific parts of a page

You can get a link to a specific part of the page, which is useful if you want to direct someone straight there, particularly if you have a lot of content on the page.

Under Viewer tools, make sure the Show anchor links is turned on, again it's on by default.

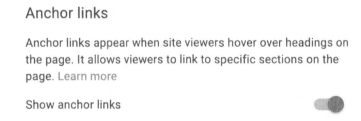

On the published page, when you hover over a header, a link icon will appear.

Click on it to copy the link.

Paste that in the browser and you will see the page address, plus an ID after the **#h** (header), which tells the browser to go to that part of the page.

sites.google.com/view/excellentenglishacademy/games#h.sjxkh6e60m0g

As we can see that's taken us to the second game on our Games page.

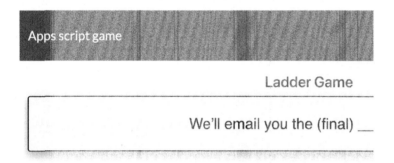

You could of course share that link in an email, messaging service, etc and it will take the person straight to where you want them to go.

Adding a custom URL

It's possible to add a custom URL to your site but you will need a registered domain to do that. You type in the domain name, then you will need to go through a verification process to check that it's yours.

www.yourdomain.com
www.excellentenglishacademy.com   Assign
This URL is not verified. Please verify your ownership.

Adding Google Analytics to your site

You can monitor the usage of your site by adding a Google Analytics tracking ID. You will need to set up a Google Analytics account to do this and get the tracking/measurement ID.

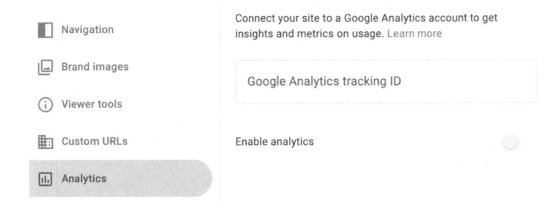

Here's an example of the information you can get from Google Analytics:

Views by Page title and screen name

No.1 Baz's bar and ...rant - Find us

2

33.33%

PAGE TITLE AND S...	VIEWS
Baz's bar a... - Find us	2
Baz's bar a... - Starters	2
Baz's bar and restaurant	1
Baz's bar a...servations	1

Adding social media links

You can add links to your social media, which has the added advantage of automatically adding common social media icons.

From Insert, click Social links.

 Social links

Add your links. Plus, you have the option of adding your own images. Then click "Insert".

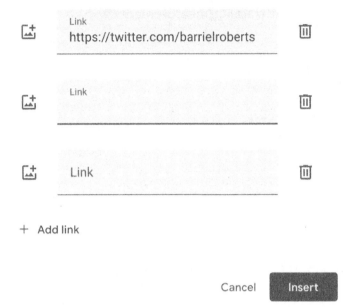

For example, I've added my Twitter link and as you can see it's added the Twitter logo. You then have the option of formatting the icon.

27 – Using templates

Sites provides you with a selection of ready-made templates, which could speed up the creation of a site.

Go to **sites.google.com**. At the top you have some templates.

And at the bottom the sites you have access to, sorted by date.

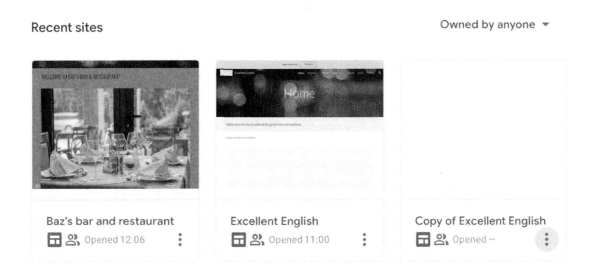

To view all the templates, click on Template gallery.

Below you will see several templates grouped by theme.

Work

Event   Help centre   Project   Team

Small business

Dog Walker   Christmas Party   Photo Portfolio   Restaurant

Salon

Click on one to create a site using that template. Here I've clicked on the Restaurant one. As you can see it's created a few pages with text and images ready to be edited.

Restaurant   **Home**   Contact us   Chef   Menu

[Restaurant name]

Write a short a tagline for your restaurant

Reservat...

28 – Customise Site Themes

When the new version of Google Sites first came out you had very limited options to style it but that's all changed and now you can use themes to not only style the way you want it but to save and share those styles between sites.

In this chapter, I'm going to show you all the options now available in themes. We're going to work with this simple website.

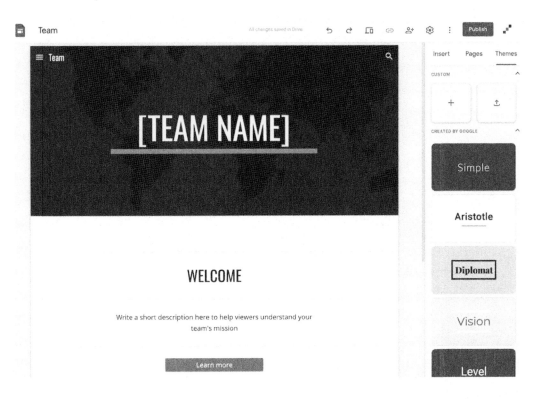

Themes lives in the top right-hand corner of the page. When you click on it you will see the pre-set themes, "Simple" to "Impression" but most importantly we know have the custom section at the top.

Here, you can either create a new theme by clicking on the plus button, or upload a theme from another site by clicking on the upload arrow button.

Creating a theme

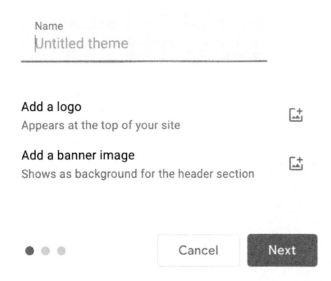

First, you give your theme a name. You then have the option to add a logo at the top of your site and a banner image, which will appear as a header background. To add the images just click on the image icons with a plus.

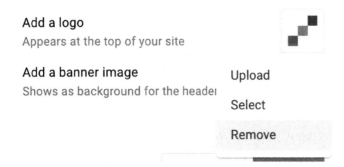

Choose "Upload" to upload an image from your computer, select to choose one from your Drive, and remove to delete an image you've already added.

← Create a theme

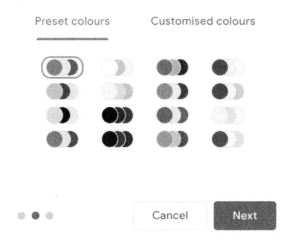

Preset colours   Customised colours

Cancel   Next

Once you've added the images you want, click Next and now you have the option of setting the main colours you want on your site. You can either use a pre-set combination or you can customise the colours yourself, maybe to match a corporate brand.

← Create a theme

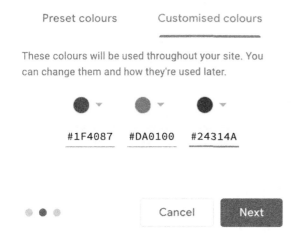

Preset colours   Customised colours

These colours will be used throughout your site. You can change them and how they're used later.

#1F4087   #DA0100   #24314A

Cancel   Next

If you choose to customise them, you can either click on one of the coloured circles, which will open up a colour palette and pick a colour form there, or if you want to create a specific colour you can enter the hexadecimal colour code. These are the three principal colours on your site.

← Create a theme

Click "Next" to select the fonts. Here, you can set the font for the titles and headers, independently from the body text. Click on the font name and pick the font you want from the drop-down list. Click Create theme to do just that.

You will see that the style of the page has already changed pretty dramatically from the original page above. You will see that the theme we just created is stored on the right-hand side menu, under Themes.

Editing a theme

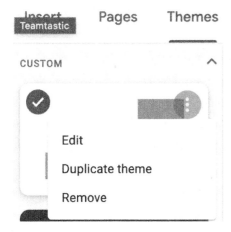

We can edit a theme and define far more options than the basic ones above. In the Themes section, click on the 3-dot menu on the theme. Then click "Edit".

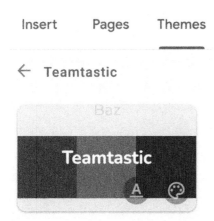

The A icon lets us edit the fonts and the palette one the colours, similar to what we saw above. But the real power is below where we can edit the colours, texts, images, navigation, and components, like buttons, in more detail.

Editing the colours

Click on the section called Colours to open it.

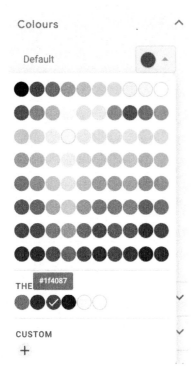

Clicking on a circle icon will open the colour palette, where you can choose either colours from the standard palette or from ones linked to the theme.

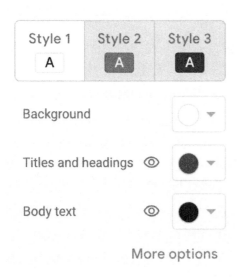

The style section lets you create up to three styles where in each style you can control the colours for the background, titles and headers, and the body text.

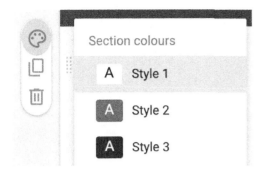

When you go to add a section, you can select one of the styles, saving you having to set the components individually every time.

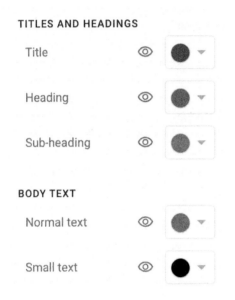

Here, I've set up the five text types and below is how they appear.

This is a heading

This is a sub-heading

This is normal text.

This is small text.

You can also click on the eye icon to see what the text will look like, so you don't have to change it. Then go to the web page to try it out.

Editing the texts

Under Colours, there are the text settings.

Here you can find a range of text settings per text style. For example, above are the settings for Normal text.

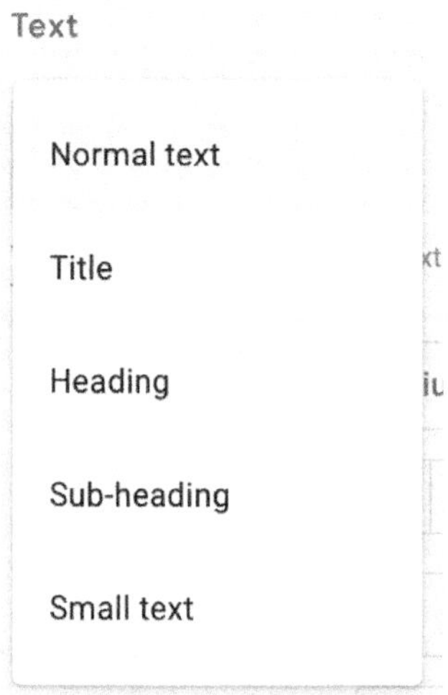

Text

Normal text

Title   xt

Heading   it

Sub-heading

Small text

Click on the drop-down menu to change the text type, then edit the settings you want.

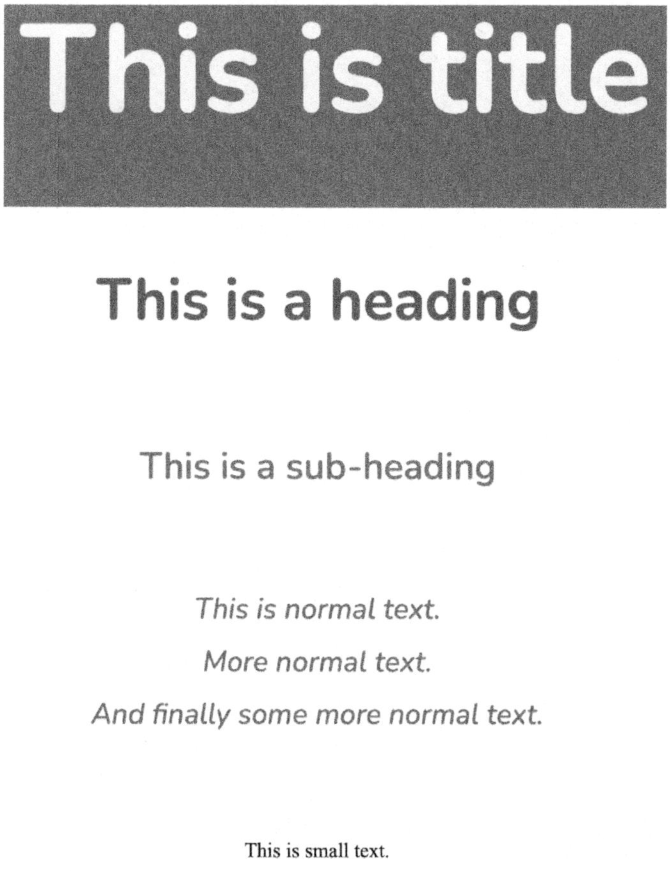

This is title

This is a heading

This is a sub-heading

This is normal text.
More normal text.
And finally some more normal text.

This is small text.

For example, above you can see you can create a wide variety of text styles.

Editing the images

Next, there are a few image settings.

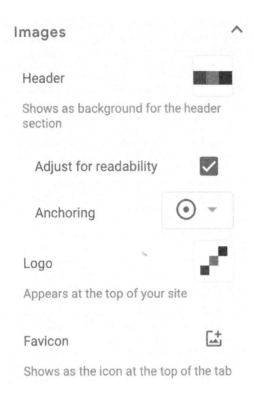

Header and logo we saw earlier in the initial edit section but here you can also adjust the readability of text over the image, plus anchor the image so that a certain side of it is shown. Useful when you have an image that is larger than the space it occupies and you want to show a certain part of it.

You can also add a favicon, which is a little icon on the browser tab.

Editing the navigation

Next, is the navigation section.

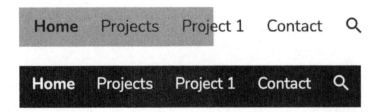

The option "Colour when scrolled" changes the background colour of the navigation bar when the page being scrolled. For example, here it changes to back. There's also the option to make it transparent.

SELECTED PAGE 👁

Top nav	Bold ▾

Side nav	Bold ▾

Next, you have the option of what a selected page looks like on the navigation bar.

The above two options are "Bold" and "Background colour". You can also highlight the active page, with a foreground colour or by underlining it. This is if you are using a top navigation bar.

Side nav	Shading ▾

Selected page colour	⚫ ▾

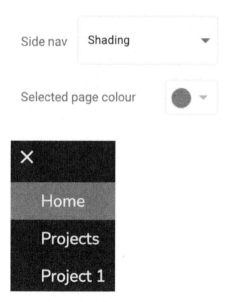

If you choose to use a side navigation bar, you also have the options "Shading", and "Line beside".

The difference between "Shading" and "Background colour", is that "Shading" will add a background colour which covers the entire width of the menu bar (as above), whereas "Background colour" just adds a background colour to the word.

Editing the components

The final part, gives you the ability to edit the buttons, dividers, links, and image carousel. There are three styles and each style has these options. Here are all the options:

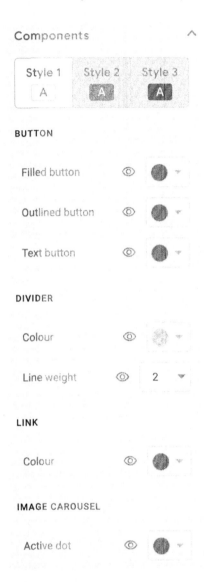

Let's look at the buttons first.

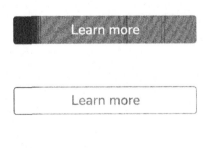

Above, we have an example of a Filled button, Outlined button, and Text button. We can add a different colour to each of them.

Next, we have two simple divider controls.

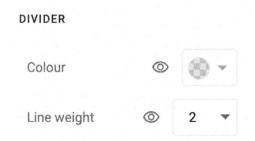

One controls the colour and the other the width of it.

Links can also have a different colour. The final option is to change the colour of the active dot on the image carousel.

Using the styles

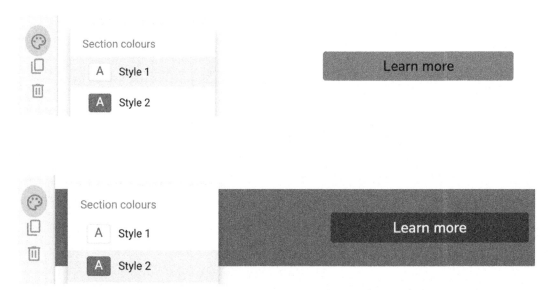

As you can see above, when we add a section, just with a click on one of the styles, we can quickly change the look of the sections, buttons, etc.

Duplicating a theme

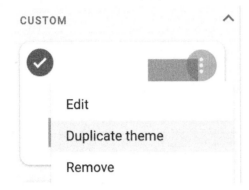

It's very easy to duplicate a theme, just click on the 3-dot menu of a theme and select Duplicate theme.

This will create a new theme card and will prompt you for a name.

Importing a theme

Click on upload a theme icon on the right.

Today

Select the Google Site with the theme you want.

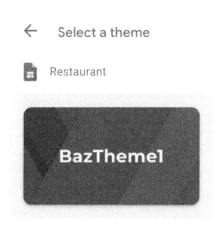

Then select the theme within that site.

This adds a theme card to the sidebar.

Clicking on it will change the current theme and look. Note, this will change the look of all the pages on your site. It's a great way to copy styles from previously made websites, to help have a standard look to them.

All the above is simple to use and can allow you create the look you want for your website.

29 – Google Sites help

I hope you have learnt a lot in this book and that you now have the tools to make some wonderful websites. If you want further help, you can find it from within your site.

Click on the 3-dot menu at the top of the page and click Help.

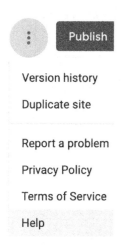

This will open the Sites help site, where you can find most answers to your questions.

How can we help you?

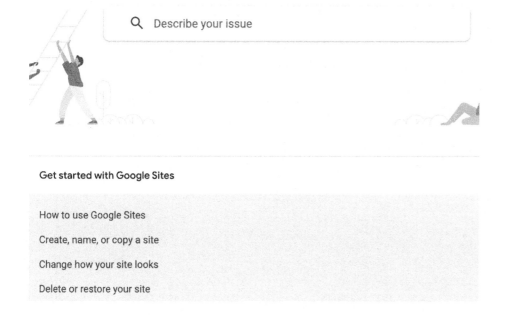

Final note from the author

I really hope this book has helped you get to know Google Sites well and that you are now able to create some wonderful websites.

If you have any questions about the content of this book, then please contact me at baz@bazroberts.com

Thank you!

Barrie "Baz" Roberts

Books and ebooks available by this author on Amazon:

Beginner's Guide to Google Drive	Beginner's Guide to Google Sheets	Beginner's Guide to Google Docs	Google Sheet Functions – A step-by-step guide
Beginner's Guide to Google Drive	Beginner's Guide to Google Sheets	Beginner's Guide to Google Docs	Google Sheet Functions A step-by-step guide
Step-by-step guide to Google Forms	Step-by-step guide to Google Sites	Step-by-step guide to Google Slides	Step-by-step guide to Google Meet
Step-by-step guide to Google Forms	Step-by-step guide to Google Sites	Step-by-step guide to Google Slides	Step-by-step guide to Google Meet

Beginner's Guide to Google Apps Script 1 - Sheets	Beginner's Guide to Google Apps Script 2 - Forms	Beginner's Guide to Google Apps Script 3 - Drive	Step-by-step Guide to Google Apps Script 4 - Documents
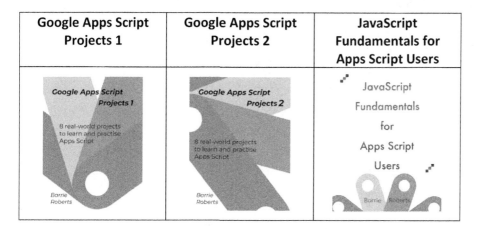

Google Apps Script Projects 1	Google Apps Script Projects 2	JavaScript Fundamentals for Apps Script Users

My website - Learning Google Workplace (G Suite) and Apps Script
https://www.bazroberts.com/

Twitter
You can also follow me on Twitter: **@barrielroberts**

Rev 4 – 2022

Appendix 1 – Setting up a Google account

Before you can create a Google Site, you will need a Google account. This is quick and easy to do, and best of all, free. Go to: https://accounts.google.com/signup

Type in your name, a username for your email address, and a password, then click Next.

Enter your date of birth and click Next.

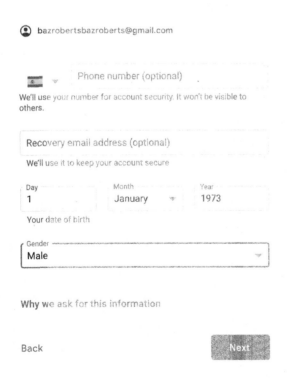

Accept the terms and conditions and click create account.

☑ I agree to the Google Terms of Service

☑ I agree to the processing of my information as described above and further explained in the Privacy Policy

Cancel   **Create Account**

Then click confirm.

Just to confirm...

This Google Account is set up to include personalisation features like **recommendations** and **personalised ads**, which are based on personal information saved to your account.

You can choose 'More Options' to change your personalisation settings and the information saved to your account.

More options   Confirm

Your account is now created! It gives you access to Gmail, Google Drive, and of course Google Sites.

Welcome, Baz Roberts

Task.

1) Summarise [key] events
(AOI) — Why is This an important moment in play as whole?) Link to Backlogue or page?

2) Explain key word in extract
in own words

Vocabulary

circle/ highlight the big ideas connected/ relevant

3)

Fate	free-will / agency	Individual vs society	family	Power	extreme forces
Love	Hate	fighting/ Conflict	duty	Society	Escape

4) Symbolism — highlight/ annotate/ complete box

5) Verbal patterns.

Printed in Great Britain by Amazon

6) Rewrite question focus.

5 methods.